the wishbone kitchen cookbook

the wishbone kitchen cookbook

Seasonal Recipes for Everyday Luxury and Elevated Entertaining

meredith hayden

with rachel holtzman

Photographs by Emma Fishman
Illustrations by Paige Spearin

contents

welcome 9

house rules and how-tos 13

some tools 14

important ingredients 17

recipe table of contents 20

secret sauces, spreads, and sprinkles 22

starters 26
salads 54
soups 78
sammies 90
veg 106
noodles 128
grains 158
surf 174
turf 196
bevs 220
baking 244
making a menu 263

acknowledgements 281

index 282

conversion tables 288

welcome

Hiiiiiii!! Welcome to *The Wishbone Kitchen Cookbook*! Can I take your coat? Are you thirsty; do you want something to drink? Water, wine, a cocktail?

Let's go sit and get comfy. So what's been going on; what's new? I wrote a book! And you're reading it right now!!! Kinda crazy, can you believe it?

Anyway, I'm so happy you're here, and I'm so excited to share these recipes with you. Whether this is our first time meeting, or we've known each other since I was selling olive oil cakes out of my parents' house (or God forbid longer): Hi, I'm Meredith!

I like to think of myself as a professional hostess. And as for you, my reader and my guest, I promise to take the utmost care of you as we venture our way through the wonderful world of Wishbone Kitchen *together.*

What you'll find here are recipes for every season of life. Yes, seasons as in spring, summer, autumn, and winter, but also like television seasons, or loosely strung together moments with new characters, plot lines, priorities, challenges, and celebrations. So no matter what season you happen to be in—within this year or within this lifetime—I promise that you'll always have the perfect thing to eat. Because when you have the perfect thing to eat, the moment becomes the memory.

how we got here

The story of Wishbone Kitchen starts with my mom, who never let a day go by without feeding us a delicious home-cooked meal. Every day after school I'd belly up to the kitchen counter, where I'd start tackling my homework. My mom would be in the kitchen, too, of course, preparing dinner and watching her favourite cooking shows. She'd expertly carve our weekly roast chicken, extracting the wishbone with ease and setting it aside for the two of us to split after dinner. My eyes would inevitably wander from my notebook to her cutting board, and an endless slew of questions would follow. My childlike curiosity and dangerously short attention span got me in a lot of trouble as a kid, but now I see these qualities as my superpower.

I've never stopped questioning why, why not, and how. Following the rules and sticking to the status quo never sat right with me. This is not an intentional act of rebellion, but something I feel to my core. This mindset is what led me to start my own private chef business at the age of twenty-three.

I was working full-time as an assistant at *Vogue*, a few months out of culinary school, and had just started working part-time with my first private chef clients. Which, at the time, was only supposed to be temporary, since my end goal was to land a job in food media. After getting a mix of rejections and non-responses from hundreds of job applications, I quickly grew more and more frustrated. As it turns out, it took a global pandemic and getting laid off from my corporate job for me to take the leap and start building my business.

"If no food media companies will hire me, I'll make my own" I said to myself. I named my imaginary (at the time) company Wishbone Kitchen, as an ode to my mother who inspired my love of home cooking. I started an Instagram page, built a website, began publishing recipes, and started booking more and more private chef gigs to pay the bills. Success did not come instantly. It rarely does. There are plenty of undocumented years of me hauling hundred pound bags of groceries through the streets of New York with negative-$200 in my checking account, a maxed-out credit card, and 117 followers on social media. I experienced countless moments where I wanted to give up and take a line-cook job for a steady paycheck. It was in these moments that I would remind myself: if Ina and Martha could turn their small catering businesses into culinary empires, then so could I.

Driven by my naive sense of invincibility, common in most early twentysomethings, and a supportive family who I knew would catch me if I fell, I persevered. I was scared shitless, navigating uncharted territory that culinary school never could've prepared me for. I think of my years as a private chef fondly. And while there are a million and one stories I could tell you, let's just say it wasn't always sunshine and hydrangeas. Mistakes were made, lessons were learned, and (luckily) the world kept on spinning.

All of this is to say, your journey in the kitchen will also be messy. You're not always going to get it right on the first try. There will be moments when you feel as though you've bitten off more than you can chew, and there will be recipes that feel like too tall of a task. **Just remember, people can do hard things and failure is a necessary part of the process.**

After dinner was over, our plates were cleared, and the kitchen was clean, my mom and I would grab on to the wishbone, we'd close our eyes, make a wish, and pull, snapping it in two. The winner being the one left with the bigger half. I know she would secretly always let me win, and this book is proof that all of my wishes have come true.

Like the name, the vibe of this book is also inspired by memories made over meals with family. Casual weeknight dinners of Shake 'N Bake. Over-the-top four-course holiday meals complete with sticky toffee pudding. Or a shared bucket of seafood pasta, devoured while we were still in our bathing suits with salty, sun-soaked skin.

Those laid-back, belly-laugh-filled suppers are my North Star because they instilled in me from a very young age that the best ingredients aren't always the most expensive, that good food doesn't have to be measured down to the last teaspoon, that luxury is a full glass and a sunset, that no moment is too small to celebrate, and that there's never a wrong time for oysters and good tequila.

Xo,
Meredith

house rules and how-tos

Now that we've got the pleasantries out of the way, it's time to get serious, so listen up. This is my cookbook, meaning my house, my rules, capiche? Disobey these rules and we're going to have some SERIOUS issues, my friends.

some basics

Always use freshly squeezed citrus—even in your cocktails, especially in your food.

Always use freshly grated cheese.

Always use fresh herbs.

NEVER use jarred garlic, like, ever.

Salt your pasta water.

take the wheel

I thought I was a great cook until I got to culinary school. Every day in class we were given a handful of recipes to prepare. Practically none of the recipes included cook times. Instead, they all read, "cook until done." This was a shock. I had never made a recipe without setting a timer. How would I know when it was done? My instructor told us, "We do not rely on timers to tell us our food is done cooking, we rely on our senses to tell us that." Let's just say I was HUMBLED. The reason for this is that there are far too many variables to account for in the kitchen to give a definitive time and temperature that will work flawlessly every time for everyone. Some chickens are bigger than others, some tomatoes are sweeter than others, some ovens run hot and some run cold, then, of course, there's human error and personal preference. So while we recipe developers can endlessly test, there still are no guarantees. That's where you come in. You must cook with your senses. Listen, watch, smell, touch, and taste your food.

When it comes to tasting and seasoning, it's always recommended to do so throughout the cooking process so that your food is evenly seasoned. To be completely honest, I never measured any of my ingredients while working as a private chef. But that is because I had lots of experience cooking with measurements and eventually developed a kind of muscle memory. While writing this cookbook, setting measurements was my biggest hurdle. I'd be testing a recipe and catch myself eye balling instead of measuring and have to start all over again.

Now, let's say by the end of the cooking process and after following the measurements and instructions to a T, you taste the dish and it's underwhelming. This is completely normal and borderline expected, and I encourage you to have the confidence to take the wheel. So, add a pinch of salt and see how you feel. Better? Add another. Getting there? Try a splash of lemon juice or a drizzle of olive oil, then taste again. It's important to note the difference a pinch of salt or a squeeze of lemon can make so you, too, can eventually build muscle memory with food. Soon enough, you'll be able to go fully off script! Because, in my world, recipes are not hard-and-fast rules. They are meant to be sources of inspiration.

some tools

Welcome to my kitchen starter pack. You don't need these exact tools, sure. But this is my cookbook, after all.

knives

Don't waste your time with an expensive knife block. Instead, focus on getting the necessities: a good chef's knife, 10 or 8 inches in size (I like Wüsthof); a serrated knife for slicing bread and tomatoes; and a paring knife for fine vegetable work.

cutting boards

It's time to get a grown-up cutting board. I am sick and tired of seeing people prep a whole ass meal on a teeny-tiny 8-inch cutting board. An 8-inch cutting board is reserved for slicing limes for cocktails. You need a larger work surface. My favourite is a 14.34 by 21.11-inch cutting board from OXO. I also love a Boos Blocks wooden cutting board.

immersion blender

Prepare for a lot of blending in this book. Involving a blender in so many recipes may seem unnecessary, but I have my reasons. The best way to use an immersion blender is in a tall, narrow container, starting the blender attachment at the bottom and slowly moving upward. For splash-free blending, tall glass measuring cups and quart containers are ideal.

quart containers

These are every cook's guilty pleasure. I always keep them on hand for storage and measuring. I mean, it's in the name and all, the tallest ones measure to 1 quart (4 cups), the medium-size ones half a quart, or a pint (2 cups), and the smallest are half a pint (1 cup). Now, abusing deli containers can be wasteful, but I use these to death. The good ones are dishwasher-safe, microwave-safe, and freezer-safe.

mandoline

Where you may fall short on knife skills, a mandoline will have your back. I love using one for getting really thin, even slices on things like radishes and cucumbers. I use it for julienning vegetables (page 70), but my favourite way to use it is to finely shave things, like the cabbage in my Cabbage and Herb Salad (page 69).

stainless-steel pots and pans

My mom has had the same 10-piece All-Clad stainless-steel set for years. They're the pots and pans that I learned how to cook with, and to this day they still look brand new. For this reason, I always recommend investing in quality stainless-steel pots and pans that, with the right care, will last you a lifetime.

microplane

I love a Microplane for zesting citrus, finely grating garlic and ginger, and grating hard cheeses like Parmesan—anytime you see an ingredient that needs to be "finely grated" do it on a Microplane! It creates the perfect consistency that can't be replicated with other graters.

roasting trays

Having multiple roasting trays is the ultimate budget-friendly kitchen luxury. Most are not too expensive and they take up very little storage space. I use them for baking, obviously, but my favourite way to use them is to organize my mise en place, or all the ingredients I've prepped in advance, especially when preparing multiple dishes at a time. In my current collection I have 2 large and 5 small roasting trays. Or in standard commercial sizing terms, I have 2 half sheets (18 by 13 by 1-inch) and five quarter sheets (13 by 9 by 1-inch). And while you might've assumed a large baking tray would be called a "full sheet," you would be wrong. This is because they were developed, and thus named, for commercial ovens which are typically much bigger than home ovens.

wire racks

Another phrase you'll see a lot in this book is "wire rack-lined roasting tray." The combination of a simple roasting tray with a wire rack placed on top is a multi-use kitchen workhorse, and another chef-y habit that I haven't been able to kick since culinary school. I use this setup as a spoon/utensil rest next to my stove top, as a roasting pan, as a cooling rack, and more. If they're both standard commercial sizing, you can buy them separately or as a set and they nest neatly on top of one another.

important ingredients

I'm exposing myself a lot throughout this book, especially my affinity for tomatoes, Calabrian chillies, and lemons, plus a few other honorable mentions. I figured I'd formally introduce you to these special-ingredient friends of mine so we can all get well acquainted with one another before we proceed.

olive oil

I love olive oil. However, the olive oil industry is inundated with so much gimmicky marketing, cross-talk, and confusing language that it's hard to decipher where you should be spending your money. First things first, extra-virgin olive oil always.

A green flag to look out for is olive oil that is single origin and clearly, and proudly, discloses where it's from. Single-origin olive oil means that the olives were all grown in one specific region. As opposed to large corporations that source olive oil from all over (for cheap) and mix them together into one big soup. My two favourite brands of olive oil are both single origin, one from Athens, Greece (P.J. Kabos) and the other from Sicily, Italy (Partanna). They are both produced by local family farms that have been making olive oil for hundreds of years, and the quality in their product shows.

In order to find your perfect olive oil match, first do some light research to find some worthy contenders. If you're someone who LOVES dark chocolate, try a "robust" olive oil. Flipside, if you prefer milk chocolate, go for a "mild" or "smooth" olive oil. Robust versus mild correlates with bitterness. Check your grocery store's return policy, then buy three different brands.

Set up a blind taste test by pouring a teaspoon of each olive oil into small bowls. Try a sip of each on their own, try dipping a piece of bread, then try dipping a piece of lettuce. Then add a pinch of salt and repeat.

You may have a clear winner, or you may like all of them. Either way, I think it's important to taste them side by side so you can taste the subtle differences. Now, you can return the olive oils you didn't like, or use them for cooking, and save your favourite for raw preparations like salad dressings, drizzling, and dipping.

Speaking of which, many cooks will tell you not to cook with extra-virgin olive oil because it has a lower smoke point than that of vegetable oil. To that I say, relax. The smoke point of olive oil ranges between 175°C to 200°C with vegetable oil coming in at about 230°C . . . and I don't know about you, but that "lower" smoke point is PLENTY high enough for most home cooking. It's not like we're working the line at a steak restaurant with ripping-hot pans. So, yes, I shall cook and fry with olive oil.

kosher salt

What's the deal! *Jerry Seinfeld voice*. But seriously, one of the most asked questions from non-recipe developers is why recipes specify "kosher" salt. And I'm here to tell the underwhelming answer and that is: math. Yes, math. Recipes call for a specific kind of salt because the salinity, or saltiness, of different salts varies. One tablespoon of kosher salt is going to be a lot less salty than one tablespoon of sea salt or iodized salt. I'm not going to get into WHY that is, because this isn't a chemistry book. What will happen if you use something other than kosher salt but you use the same measurements? Well, you're on your own, kid.

The two main brands of kosher salt are Morton Kosher and Diamond Kosher, which is my preferred brand and what I used to develop these recipes. The main difference to be aware of is the size of the salt granules. Diamond has larger granules than Morton, which means that 1 tablespoon of Morton will be saltier than 1 tablespoon of Diamond because it will have more granules. So if you're using Morton Kosher in these recipes, it's safe to say that you can halve the kosher salt measurements and adjust to taste from there.

flaky salt

I have a feeling that flaky salt is one of this decade's hot ingredients that one day we'll look back on and roll our eyes, much like we did for truffle oil in the '90s. But for now, we still love her so she stays!!! What she is is just fancy sea salt in her natural form: large pyramid-like flakes of salt. They not only add salinity, but also texture for both looks and mouthfeel! How exciting! Technically any flaky salt would work in these recipes, but my favourite is Maldon flaky salt.

peppercorns

Black vs. Pink: okay, confession!! While pink peppercorns are loved for their floral complexity, I mainly use them because they're pink and I think they're cute. I'M SORRY. So yes, you can use black peppercorns wherever you see pink peppercorns in this book.

tomatoes

If you think you hate tomatoes, fear not, I once was in your shoes. In fact, I still order cheeseburgers and sandwiches with no tomato since a lot of tomatoes are actually really bad. But a good tomato will change your life. My favourite tomato is a locally grown, in-season, heirloom tomato. Tomatoes that are not locally grown are typically harvested weeks before they're ripe to ensure they'll survive their journey through the supply chain to your grocery store. This yields a less flavourful tomato. For my go-to year-round tomato fix, I rely on cherry tomatoes, grape tomatoes, and campari tomatoes because many brands are now producing them in indoor hydroponic tomato farms, and they're just as sweet in January as they are in August.

For recipes in this book, I often call for cherry tomatoes because they are the most consistently and reliably delicious. Almost anyone, no matter where they live or what season they find themselves in, can walk into their local grocery store and buy a carton of cherry tomatoes that will meet or exceed a baseline quality level. However, it really doesn't matter the type of tomatoes you use so long as they aren't mealy, mushy, or sad. When you're making a recipe that calls for cherry tomatoes, and the farmers market has beautiful, big heirlooms, you ALWAYS have my blessing to swap. Same goes in reverse. If a recipe calls for heirloom tomatoes but they're nowhere to be found, go with whatever looks best. It's really not that serious. But whatever you do, season your damn tomatoes!!!!! Whether they're going in a salad, in a sandwich, or on a piece of toast, show them some love (in this case, love = salt, pepper, extra-virgin olive oil), and I promise they will love you back.

calabrian chillies

You may read this book and think, based on the frequency that I use these jarred Italian chillies, that I have some vested interest in the Calabrian chilli business. I'm just obsessed. Calabrian chillies, named after their region of origin—Calabria, Italy—have a bright, fruity flavour profile rather than an intense burning heat found in many other chillies. You'll see them called for in this book as "chopped Calabrian chillies" and that's because I am not looking for a fresh chilli pepper, I'm looking for the jarred stuff that often comes already chopped. You can also find jarred whole Calabrian chillies and hand chop them at home, but this can cause quite a mess. Depending on the brand, they may also be labeled crushed Calabrian chillies, bomba di Calabria hot pepper sauce, bomba Calabrese, peperoncini piccanti, or spicy Calabrian pepper spread. They're typically preserved in a heavenly mixture of extra-virgin olive oil, vinegar, salt, and sometimes basil that only enhances their flavours even more. If you can't get your hands on Calabrians, some similar substitutes that can be swapped in a pinch include gochujang, sambal, sriracha, or just plain crushed red pepper flakes.

hot honey

As a die-hard savoury person, I can attest that a dash of sweetness and a hint of spice elevate almost any salty dish. Hot honey has the convenience of both sweet and spicy in one, but if you don't have hot honey you can substitute with regular honey and maybe a pinch of chilli flakes. Speaking of . . .

chilli flakes

Your standard "crushed red pepper flakes" are the most common chilli flake found in grocery stores, but I encourage you to experiment with other types, such as gochugaru, Espelette, ancho, guajillo, and smoked chilli flakes. The flavour will vary slightly, but rarely enough to make them un-substitutable.

citrus

You all should be seasoning food with more acid (seasoning doesn't just mean salt and pepper), and citrus fruits, lemons specifically, are my acid of choice. If you have ever wondered why the world unanimously adores hot sauce, it's not because we all love painfully spicy food. It's because of acid; the main ingredient in most hot sauces is vinegar. The reason it makes food taste so good is because the acidic edge cuts through fatty, salty food (like bacon, egg, and cheese on a bagel). So it balances but also enhances the flavours in a dish, much like salt. When you're preparing yourself a nice meal, however, dousing it in hot sauce isn't exactly a good look, and that's where lemons come in. I finish almost all of my food with a sprinkle of lemon zest and a squeeze of lemon juice. I recommend zesting your citrus directly over your food—this way the flavourful oils from the citrus end up in your dish and not on your cutting board.

herbs

There are two main categories of culinary herbs: grassy and woody. Grassy herbs resemble, well, grass. Think chives, parsley, coriander, tarragon, dill, sage, and basil. Grassy herbs should ALWAYS be used in their fresh form, never dried. Then woody herbs have a hard wood-like stem at their base, such as rosemary, thyme, oregano, and marjoram. These are great both dried and fresh. Then there's mint, technically a woody herb but should be treated like a grassy herb, and always used fresh. I am an herb enthusiast as you will quickly find out upon flipping through this book.

recipe table of contents

STARTERS

Heirloom Crab Cocktail 28

Oysters Parm 31

Stracciatella with Marinated Sungolds 35

Really Good Guac 36

Hot Crab Dip 39

Ricotta with Fried Garlic 40

Calabrian Tuna Tartare Toast 43

Caesar Crudités 44

Oysters with Yuzu Kosho Mignonette 47

Bacon Bays 48

Crispy Caviar Potatoes 51

Crushed Olive Spread 52

SALADS

Italian Chopped with Buffalo Mozzarella 56

Squash Ribbons with Pistachio and Pecorino 59

Lobster Avocado Salad 60

THE Green Salad 65

Blueberry BBQ Grilled Chicken Salad 66

Cabbage and Herb Salad 69

Big Fat Greek Salad with Souvlaki-ish Chicken 73

PLT Salad 74

Radicchio with Hazelnuts and Brown Butter Vinaigrette 77

SOUPS

Ribollita 80

Lobster Bisque 83

Green Garlic and Ginger Chicken Soup 87

Chicken Khao Soi 88

SAMMIES

Ultimate Italian 93

Hot Buttered Lobster Rolls 94

Chicken Cutlet Club 97

Green Curry Katsu Sando 98

Piri-Piri Chicken Sandwiches 101

Pork Sausage Burgers 102

Steak "Tartare" Sandwich 105

VEG

Blanched Spring Veg 108

Grilled Summer Veg 111

Roasted Winter Veg 112

Brown Buttered Broccoli 115

Tomatoes and Corn 116

Asparagus Fries with Feta 119

Roasted Broccoli with Caper Butter 120

Chilli-Braised Cauliflower 123

Duck Fat Potatoes 124

A Good Mash 127

NOODLES

Bucatini and Meatballs 131

Spicy Squash Pasta 135

Ziti alla Zozzona 137

Short Rib Bolognese 141

Broccoli Cavatelli 143

Baked Crab Mac and Cheese 147

Lobster Capellini 148

Pink Lemon Pasta 151

Sungold Tomato Pasta 152

Wok Lobster 155

Lemongrass Chicken & Rice Noodle Salad 156

GRAINS

Crab Fried Rice 161

Farro Broccoli Salad 162

Tomato and Spot Prawn Paella 165

Mom's Pilaf 169

Herby Rice and Radish Salad 170

Pecorino Polenta 173

SURF

Nantucket Clambake 176

Tomato Butter Baked Cod 180

Chive Crab Cakes 183

Scampi Shrimp 185

Fish Tacos 189

Crispy Fish with Citrus Salad 190

Butterflied Branzino 193

Slow-Roasted Salmon with Ponzu and Sesame Chilli Crunch 194

TURF

Not My Mom's Roast Chicken 199

Shake 'N Bake Chicken with Hot Honey Tomatoes 203

Boyfriend Roast Chicken with Pan-Sauce Potatoes 204

Duck Lettuce Wraps 207

Pork Tacos with Roasted Peach Salsa 210

Harissa Pitas with Feta and Cucumber 215

Porterhouse with Jammy Tomatoes 216

Balsamic Braised Short Ribs 219

BEVS

Dirty Martini with Blue Cheese-Stuffed Olives 223

Pickled Pepper Martini 224

Lambrusco Negroni 227

Spicy Salty Ranch Water 228

Picante Piña 231

Cucumber Melon Spritzes 232

Passion Fruit Mezcalita 235

Boozy Blueberry Basil Lemonade 236

Jalapeño Michelada 241

Garden Mere-y 242

BAKING

Heirloom Tomato Galette 246

Cathead Biscuits and Blueberry Jam 249

Olive Oil Cake with Peaches and Cream 251

Deconstructed Pie Sundaes 255

S'mores Ice Cream Pie 256

Sticky Toffee Pudding 259

MAKING A MENU

Winter Holiday 267

Birthday 268

Taco Party 271

Summer Clambake 272

Country Club 275

Pasta Party 276

Manifesting the Med 279

secret sauces, spreads, and sprinkles

I love efficiency, and I find that the best way to achieve it in the kitchen is to repeat recipes. Making the same thing over and over again is essential to gaining confidence and I recommend it to aspiring home cooks and professional cooks alike. This doesn't have to mean dinner looks the same every night. What it could mean is having a handful of sauces, spreads, and sprinkles that you can use as the foundation for a variety of dishes. This also means you prep a double batch of something, freeze half, and save your future self time and effort down the road. Here are some of my go-to special sauces, spreads, and sprinkles in the book!

CLASSIC RED SAUCE
(PAGE 132)

SALSA VERDE(S)
PARSLEY CAPER SALSA VERDE
(PAGE 193)

CITRUS CORIANDER SALSA VERDE
(PAGE 190)

PARSLEY TARRAGON SALSA VERDE
(PAGE 199)

TOMATILLO SALSA VERDE
(PAGE 213)

BASIL PARSLEY PESTO
(PAGE 144)

BUTTERMILK RANCH
(PAGE 74)

BALSAMIC VINAIGRETTE
(PAGE 56)

CHAMPAGNE VINAIGRETTE
(PAGE 65)

LEMON AÏOLI
(PAGE 43)

TOMATO NUOC CHAM
(PAGE 70)

SESAME CHILLI CRUNCH
(PAGE 136)

QUICK-PICKLED SHALLOTS
(PAGE 74)

HARISSA SEASONING BLEND
(PAGE 112)

TOASTED GARLIC PANKO
(PAGE 31)

BLUEBERRY JAM
(PAGE 250)

starters

HEIRLOOM CRAB COCKTAIL

1 cup cherry tomatoes, plus more thinly sliced, for garnish

1 mini cucumber, roughly chopped

1 small jalapeño, half roughly chopped, half thinly sliced for garnish

½ small shallot, peeled and roughly chopped

1 tablespoon white wine vinegar, plus more as needed

8 ounces white crabmeat

1 lemon, zested and halved

Microgreens, for serving

Extra-virgin olive oil

Kosher and flaky salt

Serves 4 to 6

This dish reimagines what a "seafood cocktail" can be. Rather than slathering it in mayo or dunking it in horseradish-y tomato ketchup, tender, sweet chunks of crab get the royal treatment, thanks to fresh tomato gazpacho and a drizzle of your finest olive oil. I love serving this for guests since all of the prep is done ahead of time, and it comes together in minutes.

MAKE THE GAZPACHO: Combine the whole tomatoes, the cucumber, chopped jalapeño, shallot, vinegar, 1 tablespoon olive oil, and ¼ teaspoon kosher salt in a blender and blend until smooth. Taste and adjust the seasoning with more salt and/or vinegar, if needed. Transfer to an airtight container and refrigerate for at least 6 hours, but preferably overnight.

PREP THE CRAB: Drain off any liquid in the container. Transfer the crabmeat to a cutting board or plate and comb through for any rogue pieces of shell and cartilage to discard. Pat dry with kitchen towels.

ASSEMBLE AND SERVE: In a medium bowl, combine the crabmeat with the thinly sliced jalapeño, lemon zest, a drizzle of olive oil, a squeeze of lemon juice, and a pinch of flaky salt. Gently fold together to combine.

Divide the gazpacho among individual serving bowls. Pile the crab mixture in the centre and garnish with sliced cherry tomatoes and jalapeños, another drizzle of olive oil, and microgreens.

OYSTERS PARM

For the Tomato Butter Sauce

1 stick (8 tablespoons) unsalted butter

1 cup cherry tomatoes, halved

2 tablespoons tomato paste

2 medium garlic cloves, peeled and finely grated

1 teaspoon chopped Calabrian chillies or crushed red pepper flakes

½ lemon, zested

Kosher salt

For the Oysters

24 medium to large oysters

⅓ cup Toasted Garlic Panko (recipe follows)

Freshly grated Parm, for serving

Fresh basil leaves, for serving

Lemon wedges, for serving

Toasted bread, for serving

Serves 4 to 6

These oysters-Rockefeller-meets-chicken-Parm beauties (dare I say Oysters Parm-efeller . . .) are loaded with fresh and buttery tomato sauce, a dusting of Parm, and crispy panko. Grilling the oysters rather than barbecueing (my second favourite oyster cooking method) allows you to seamlessly cook off big batches (every party host's dream) without sweating over an open flame.

Preheat the grill to high and set the top oven rack about 4 inches from the grill.

MAKE THE TOMATO BUTTER SAUCE: In a small saucepan over medium heat, melt the butter. Add the tomatoes, tomato paste, garlic, chillies, lemon zest, and ¼ teaspoon of salt. Simmer until the tomatoes have softened, about 5 minutes, using the back of a spoon to smash some of the tomatoes to release their juices as they cook. Turn off the heat and set the sauce aside.

PREP THE OYSTERS: Thoroughly clean the oyster shells under cold running water and then use an oyster knife to shuck them. If you don't have an oyster knife, see page 32 for instructions on how to open them by a quick grilling.

ASSEMBLE AND BAKE: Arrange the shucked oysters on a wire rack-lined roasting tray, and prop them up with kitchen foil as demonstrated on page 32. Top each oyster with a spoonful of buttery tomato sauce, a sprinkle of toasted garlic panko, and a dusting of freshly grated Parm. Transfer to the oven and grill until bubbling and golden brown, 3 to 5 minutes.

TO SERVE: Transfer the oysters to a serving tray, or serve right from the roasting tray. Top with more freshly grated Parm and basil leaves and serve with lemons and toasted bread.

TOASTED GARLIC PANKO

2 tablespoons olive oil

1 tablespoon unsalted butter

1 medium garlic clove, grated

1 cup panko breadcrumbs

Kosher salt

Makes 1 cup

TOAST THE PANKO: Heat a large frying pan over medium heat and add the olive oil and butter. When the butter has melted, stir in the garlic and cook until fragrant, about 30 seconds, then add the panko and toss to coat. Toast, stirring occasionally, until the breadcrumbs are golden, 5 to 7 minutes. Turn off the heat, add a pinch of salt, and transfer the breadcrumbs to a bowl and set aside.

Store the breadcrumbs in an airtight container in the fridge for up to 1 week.

shuck your oysters in the oven

Line a rimmed roasting tray with a wire rack. Depending on the size and shape of your oysters, the wire rack may be sufficient to secure them. If they tilt forward or sideways, you'll need to prop them up so the juice inside won't spill out when they open. To do so, tear off a few pieces of kitchen foil, shape them into tubes that are the same length as the roasting tray, and wedge the foil tubes underneath the oysters, as pictured below. Secure the oysters by gently pressing them into the foil to create a little pocket for each to rest in. Place the pan under the preheated grill and grill just until the oysters pop open, about 4 minutes.

Let the oysters cool slightly before removing the top shell with your hands, taking care not to let any liquid spill out. Use an oyster knife or a spoon to release the oyster meat from the bottom shell.

STRACCIATELLA WITH MARINATED SUNGOLDS

2 cups Sungold tomatoes, or any cherry tomatoes, halved

½ small shallot, peeled and finely chopped

⅓ cup extra-virgin olive oil, plus more for toasting

1 teaspoon freshly ground pink or black pepper

8 ounces stracciatella cheese, store-bought or homemade (recipe follows)

Sourdough bread, or any crusty loaf, cut into ½-inch slices

Flaky salt

Serves 4 to 6

This dish is proof that a little attention to detail can go a long way. The star is the Sungolds, a variety of cherry tomatoes known for its sweetness and sunny yellowish-orange hue. Here they're drenched in a shallot marinade and perfectly paired with stracciatella cheese, a magical combination of mozzarella curds mixed with fresh cream. It's famously found in the centre of burrata cheese, but also can exist solo as it does here. Naturally we need some crusty bread to sop up all of that goodness, and that my friends is the perfect appetizer.

Preheat the oven to 200°C.

MARINATE THE TOMATOES: In a medium bowl, toss together the Sungolds and shallots with the olive oil, 2 teaspoons flaky salt, and freshly ground peppercorns. Let the mixture marinate in the fridge, covered, for at least an hour or up to 24 hours.

PREP THE STRACCIATELLA: Put the stracciatella in a fine-mesh sieve and allow it to drain for a minute or two. This will remove excess moisture, making it less runny on the plate and easier, i.e. less messy, to serve and eat.

TOAST THE BREAD: Arrange the bread in a single layer on a roasting tray and drizzle both sides with olive oil. Bake, turning once, until golden brown, about 5 minutes per side.

SERVE: Spoon the stracciatella and tomatoes into a shallow bowl or rimmed serving plate and drizzle with the remaining marinade and a sprinkle of flaky salt. Serve with the toasted bread.

HOMEMADE STRACCIATELLA

8 ounces fresh mozzarella or buffalo mozzarella cheese

½ cup double cream

Kosher salt

If you can't find stracciatella at the store, or you'd rather overachieve, you can make your own.

In a small bowl, tear the mozzarella into 1-inch pieces. Stir in the double cream and a pinch of salt. Let the mixture sit for at least 4 hours or overnight in the refrigerator. Adjust the consistency by straining off any excess liquid before serving.

REALLY GOOD GUAC

½ cup packed fresh coriander leaves and stems, plus more for garnish

1 small jalapeño, roughly chopped

1 lime, zested and juiced (about 1 tablespoon)

1 medium garlic clove, peeled and roughly chopped

4 medium ripe avocados

½ small white onion, peeled and finely chopped (about ½ cup)

½ teaspoon kosher salt

Thinly sliced tomatoes and jalapeños, for garnish

Serves 4 to 6

Why settle for a lacklustre and flavourless guac experience? Demand better from your guac! That's why we're making a super-concentrated, spicy, coriander-y, lime-y puree that's folded into the avocado to taste (seriously, taste as you go so you can discover your version of very good guac) to ensure that all bites are really good bites.

PREP THE PUREE: Use an immersion blender to blend the coriander, jalapeño, lime juice, and garlic until smooth. Set aside. (You can also just finely chop the ingredients by hand.)

PREP THE AVOCADOS: Cut the avocados in half and remove the stones. Roughly chop into a medium dice and transfer to a large mixing bowl. Use a potato masher or a large fork to mash until you achieve your desired consistency.

MAKE THE GUAC: Use a rubber spatula to fold in the onion, salt, and about half of the coriander mixture. Taste and add more of the coriander mixture and/or salt as desired. I like my guac *very* herby and *very* acidic, so I use all of it. But for a more classic mild guac flavour, you may want to hold back.

SERVE: Plate in a shallow bowl. Garnish with thinly sliced tomatoes, jalapeños, and coriander.

To store, squeeze more lime juice over the top and tightly cover by placing cling film directly on the surface. Keep in the fridge for up to 3 days.

HOT TIP

For a diced avocado hack, place a wire rack over a medium bowl and place an unpeeled avocado half on the rack, flesh side down. Gently push the avocado through the rack. Once you get into a rhythm you can process avocados in half the time as hand chopping.

HOT CRAB DIP

1 pound white crabmeat

8 ounces cream cheese, at room temperature

4 ounces extra-sharp Cheddar cheese, freshly grated (about 1 cup)

¼ cup mayonnaise

¼ cup jarred pimiento peppers, drained and finely chopped

2 tablespoons chopped Calabrian chillies

1 lemon, zested, plus 1 lemon, cut into wedges, for serving

1 teaspoon Old Bay Seasoning

½ teaspoon kosher salt

½ cup thinly sliced spring onions (white and green parts; about 3 spring onions), plus more for serving

Celery, Ritz crackers, or crisps, for serving

Serves 6 to 8

I'd like to formally thank crabmeat for making hot cream cheese a class act. As one of my favourite appetizer categories, hot cream cheese was due for a glow up, and this lightened, brightened version is the answer. In the summer it feels fresh and beachy; in winter it leans surf-and-turf steakhouse vibes—it's truly a dip for all seasons.

Preheat the oven to 180°C.

PREP THE CRAB: Drain off any liquid from the container and transfer the crabmeat to a cutting board or plate. Comb through the meat and remove any rogue pieces of shell and cartilage. Pat dry with kitchen towels.

MAKE THE DIP: In a large bowl, combine the cream cheese, Cheddar cheese, mayo, pimientos, chillies, lemon zest, Old Bay, and salt. Mix until well combined. Add ½ cup spring onions and the crabmeat to the cream cheese mixture and gently mix until just combined. Be careful not to break up the large chunks of crabmeat.

Transfer the mixture to a small baking dish and bake until the dip is golden brown and bubbly, about 30 minutes.

SERVE: Garnish with spring onions and serve with celery, crackers, and/or crisps for dipping, and lemon wedges.

PIMIENTO-ISH CHEESE

8 ounces cream cheese, at room temperature

8 ounces extra-sharp Cheddar cheese, freshly grated (about 2 cups)

¼ cup mayo

¼ cup jarred pimiento peppers, drained and finely chopped

2 tablespoons chopped Calabrian chillies

Crackers, crudités, or bread for serving

Serves 6

Hold the crab and double the Cheddar and you've got my pimiento(ish) cheese, the quintessential Southern spread. This recipe has been approved by my opinionated Southern mother.

MAKE THE DIP: In a medium bowl, stir together the cream cheese, Cheddar cheese, mayo, pimientos, and Calabrian chillies. Serve as a dip with crackers and crudités, on a burger, or simply sandwiched between two slices of white bread.

HOT TIP
If you don't have jarred pimiento peppers, you can use jarred or fresh roasted red peppers instead.

RICOTTA WITH FRIED GARLIC

¼ cup extra-virgin olive oil, plus more as needed

6 medium garlic cloves, peeled and very thinly sliced

1 tablespoon fresh thyme leaves

16 ounces full-fat ricotta cheese (about 2 cups)

Hot honey, for drizzling

Sourdough bread, or any crusty loaf, cut into ½-inch slices

Flaky salt

Serves 4

This dish was born out of frustration at the cost of assembling a half-decent cheese board. When sourcing a variety of cheeses, meats, and spreads, you can accidentally find yourself spending a week's worth of grocery budget on a damn appetizer. I'm sorry, but no friendship is worth that unnecessary financial strain. Intro my girl, ricotta. She's affordable and takes very little dressing up to become dinner-party ready. Just throw in some fresh thyme, hot honey, and crispy garlic and call it a day.

Preheat the oven to 200°C.

FRY THE GARLIC: Place a fine-mesh sieve over a medium heatproof bowl and set aside. In a small saucepan, combine the olive oil and sliced garlic. Stir to separate any slices that are stuck together so that all the garlic slices are coated with oil. The garlic should be submerged in oil, so add more oil if necessary.

Place the pan over medium heat and cook until the oil just begins to bubble. Continue cooking until the garlic turns light golden, or "blond", 3 to 5 minutes. Add the thyme, cook for 30 seconds, then immediately pour the mixture through the sieve.

Transfer the garlic chips and thyme to a kitchen towel-lined plate and season with a pinch of flaky salt. Set aside to cool. Reserve the garlic-infused oil for serving.

TOAST THE BREAD: Arrange the bread in a single layer on a roasting tray and drizzle both sides with olive oil. Bake, turning once, until golden brown, about 5 minutes per side.

ASSEMBLE AND SERVE: Use a large spoon to dollop and swirl the ricotta onto a serving plate. Spoon over a few tablespoons of the garlic oil and top with the crispy garlic slices and thyme. Drizzle with hot honey and finish with a generous sprinkle of flaky salt. Serve with toasted bread.

HOT TIP
Any extra garlic-infused oil can be used in salad dressings, soups, or any sauce you like.

CALABRIAN TUNA TARTARE TOAST

¾ pound high-quality tuna

Sourdough bread, or any crusty loaf, cut into 1-inch slices

1 lemon

1 tablespoon chopped Calabrian chillies

3 tablespoons finely chopped fresh chives

Lemon aïoli (recipe follows)

Extra-virgin olive oil, for frying and finishing

Flaky salt

Serves 4 to 6

Think of this as Japanese spicy tuna crispy rice that went on a luxurious coastal Italian vacation. The tuna is diced and tossed with Calabrian chillies and then heaped over a bright Lemon Aïoli. The real unsung hero is the bread, pan-fried so it gets a golden crispy crust while maintaining a soft, pillowy interior. It's a showstopper, either as an appetizer or built into a meal by adding a side of greens.

PREP THE TUNA: Using a very sharp knife, cut the tuna into ½-inch-thick cubes. Transfer the tuna to a medium bowl, cover, and refrigerate until you're ready to serve.

FRY THE BREAD: Line a roasting tray with a wire rack and set aside.

Heat a large frying pan over medium-high heat. Add enough olive oil to coat the bottom of the pan with about a ⅛ inch of oil and heat until it shimmers. Carefully add the bread, working in batches, and fry until golden brown on both sides, about 2 minutes per side. Add more oil between batches as needed. Transfer the bread to the wire rack to cool.

DRESS THE TUNA: Remove the tuna from the fridge. Add the zest of half a lemon, the Calabrian chillies, chives, a pinch of flaky salt, and a generous glug of olive oil. Mix to combine, taste, and add more chillies if you want more heat.

Add a smear of aïoli to each toast and top with the tuna mixture. Finish with more lemon zest, and serve immediately.

LEMON AÏOLI

1 medium egg yolk

1 small garlic clove, peeled and finely grated

1 teaspoon Dijon mustard

¼ cup extra-virgin olive oil

¼ cup vegetable oil

¼ teaspoon kosher salt

1 lemon

White wine vinegar (optional)

Makes about 2 cups

If you want to make the aïoli in the food processor, you can—just double the recipe.

In a large bowl, whisk to thoroughly combine the egg yolk, garlic, and mustard. Whisking constantly, very slowly stream in the olive and vegetable oils. Continue whisking until the mixture has thickened and emulsified. Add the salt. Zest half of the lemon directly into the bowl, then halve the lemon and add the juice from 1 lemon half, or more to taste, and mix well. For a more acidic aïoli, add a splash of white wine vinegar. Store in an airtight container in the fridge until ready to use.

CAESAR CRUDITÉS

8 garlic cloves, peeled, plus 1 garlic clove, peeled and finely grated

1 lemon, zested and juiced (about 2 to 3 tablespoons), plus 1 lemon, thinly sliced for serving

1 (2-ounce) tin flat anchovies in olive oil, one finely minced and the rest left whole

½ cup Lemon Aïoli (see page 43) or mayo

½ cup plain full-fat Greek yogurt

1 ounce Parmesan cheese, finely grated (about ¼ cup), plus shaved Parm for serving

Assorted veg, such as sliced radishes, cucumber, endive, and Little Gem lettuce, for serving

Crackers and crostini, for serving

Extra-virgin olive oil

Kosher salt, flaky salt, and freshly ground black pepper

Serves 4 to 6

Caesar salad should be eaten with your hands. My supporting evidence: The consistency of a proper Caesar dressing is super thick—less than ideal for delicately coating tender greens but more than ideal for dipping. So I'm bringing my salad to the dressing. It's the grown-up version of pre-sliced celery and ranch platters, best served with a sidecar of anchovies.

MAKE THE GARLIC CONFIT: In a small saucepan, combine the 8 whole garlic cloves and enough olive oil to cover. Heat over medium heat until the oil is simmering, then adjust to low heat, and cook until the garlic is golden brown and soft, 30 to 45 minutes. Using a slotted spoon, transfer the garlic to a cutting board. Transfer the oil into a heatproof container and set both aside to cool.

MAKE THE DIP: Roughly chop the confit garlic, then smash it into a paste using the broad side of your knife or a fork. Transfer to a bowl along with 1 tablespoon of confit garlic oil, the raw grated garlic, zest from ½ of the lemon, 1 tablespoon of the lemon juice, and the chopped anchovy. Whisk until homogeneous. Add the lemon aïoli, yogurt, grated Parm, ¼ teaspoon kosher salt, and lots of black pepper. Whisk to combine. Taste and adjust with additional kosher salt, pepper, and/or lemon juice as needed.

ASSEMBLE AND SERVE: Transfer the dip to a serving bowl. Drizzle with more garlic oil and top with a pinch of flaky salt and a crack of pepper. Dip and spread onto crackers and veg, top with an anchovy, shaved Parm, and sliced lemon for a perfect Caesar-y bite.

HOT TIP
If you're making homemade aïoli for this recipe, use the leftover oil from the garlic confit in place of plain olive oil for an extra garlicky flavour. Just be sure to allow the oil to come to room temp before using.

OYSTERS WITH YUZU KOSHO MIGNONETTE

For the Yuzu Kosho Mignonette

1 small shallot, peeled and finely chopped

3 tablespoons unseasoned rice vinegar

1 lime, zested and juiced (about 1 tablespoon)

1 teaspoon yuzu kosho paste

½ teaspoon fish sauce

For Assembly

Crushed ice, for serving

24 oysters on the half shell

1 mini cucumber, finely diced

Lime wedges, for serving

Serves 4 to 6

I believe putting cocktail sauce on raw oysters is a crime. Mignonette, on the other hand, is a high-acid splash that brings a briny oyster to life. This version utilizes one of my favourite ingredients, yuzu kosho, a Japanese fermented citrus chilli paste that strikes the perfect balance of funky, salty, spicy, and citrus-y. You can find it at most Japanese grocery stores, or order it online. If you don't have yuzu kosho, you can sub finely grated jalapeño or serrano peppers and extra lime zest. You won't get the same fermented depth of the yuzu kosho, but the fish sauce will help make up for it.

MAKE THE YUZU KOSHO MIGNONETTE: In a small bowl, whisk together the shallot, vinegar, lime zest and juice, yuzu kosho paste, and fish sauce. Cover the bowl and refrigerate for at least 30 minutes before using or up to 2 days.

SERVE: Arrange the oysters on a serving platter or over crushed ice. Top each with a spoonful of mignonette and finely diced cucumber. Serve with lime wedges.

HOT TIP
Shucking oysters is a great life skill and a cool party trick, but don't ruin your day over it. There's no shame in asking your fishmonger to shuck them for you.

CLASSIC MIGNONETTE

1 small shallot, peeled and finely chopped

¼ cup red wine vinegar

¼ teaspoon kosher salt

¼ teaspoon freshly ground pink or black pepper

In a small bowl, whisk together the shallot, vinegar, salt, and pepper. Cover, and refrigerate for at least 30 minutes before using or up to 1 month.

BACON BAYS

4 thin slices of prosciutto

2 dozen fresh sea scallops or Nantucket bay scallops

½ stick (4 tablespoons) salted butter

1 medium garlic clove, peeled and finely grated

1 lemon, zested and halved, plus 1 lemon, cut into wedges, for serving

¼ cup finely chopped fresh chives

Extra-virgin olive oil

Kosher salt

Serves 4

HOT TIP
For an extra-golden brown sear, lightly dust the presentation side of your sea scallops with plain flour, tapping off any excess, before frying.

HOT TIP
Nantucket bay scallops are smaller than sea scallops. So when substituting, adjust the quantity as you see fit.

This recipe is named after a quintessential Nantucket dish of bacon-wrapped bay scallops. Nantucket bay scallops are harvested from the calm waters of the Nantucket Sound and are about a third of the size of standard sea scallops. Wrapping them in bacon and deep frying them, while delicious, feels like an injustice. Instead, I prefer to let the sweet flavour shine in a light lemon butter sauce with a sprinkling of crispy prosciutto. And since fresh bay scallops are highly seasonal and hyper-regional in availability (sad), I've done us all a favor and provided instructions for preparing this dish using standard sea scallops.

Preheat the oven to 200°C.

CRISP UP THE PROSCIUTTO: Line a roasting tray with parchment paper. Arrange the prosciutto in a single layer, leaving space between each slice. Bake until golden and crisp, about 5 minutes. Set aside to cool, then finely chop.

PREP THE SCALLOPS: Pat them dry with a kitchen towel.

SEAR THE SCALLOPS: Heat a large sauté pan over medium-high heat. Add enough olive oil to coat the bottom, 1 to 2 tablespoons. You'll know the pan is ready for the scallops once the oil begins to shimmer. Just before adding them to the pan, season the scallops with salt. Working in batches, sear the scallops on one side, leaving them undisturbed until they develop a golden brown crust, 3 to 5 minutes for sea scallops or 30 to 60 seconds for bay scallops.

Without searing the second side, transfer the scallops to a roasting tray, seared side up. Repeat with the remaining scallops, adding more oil to the pan as needed.

MAKE THE SAUCE: Pour off any excess oil. Return the pan to medium-high heat and add the butter. When the butter has melted, add the garlic and 1 teaspoon of the lemon zest. Cook until fragrant, about 60 seconds.

FINISH THE SCALLOPS: Return all the scallops to the pan, seared side up and finish cooking in the hot butter for about 1 minute, basting them with the sauce as they cook. Turn off the heat and finish the scallops with the juice of half of a lemon and half of the chives.

TO SERVE: Transfer the scallops to a serving dish, seared side up, and spoon over the butter sauce. Top with more lemon zest, the remaining chives, and the chopped prosciutto.

CRISPY CAVIAR POTATOES

1 pound small yellow potatoes, about 1½ to 2 inches each

3 tablespoons unsalted butter, melted

Crème fraîche, for serving

Finely chopped fresh chives, for serving

Caviar or fish roe, for serving

Kosher salt

Serves 4 to 6

We didn't go out to restaurants very much when I was young, but when we did we went to our fair share of kid-friendly, tavern-like sports bars, most of them with menus that didn't stray too far from a familiar path. It was during these times when my brother and I developed a strong affection for fried potato skins. For those unfamiliar, these are crispy, hollowed-out baked potato boats filled with cheese and sour cream and topped with bacon. Well, I'm a grown up now (or at least pretending to be) so I've swapped my Blue's Clues PJs for silk sets and my bacon bits for caviar. Not actually, tho, I'll still knock back potato skins like it's '05.

BOIL THE POTATOES: In a large pot, cover the potatoes with an inch of cold water and season with a teaspoon of salt. Bring the potatoes to a boil. Cook until they can be easily pierced with the tip of a sharp knife, about 10 minutes. Drain well and set aside until they are cool enough to comfortably handle.

Preheat the oven to 230°C. Use the fan setting or an air fryer if available.

PREP THE POTATOES AND FILLING: When the potatoes are cool enough to handle, slice them in half. Use a small spoon to carefully carve out a small divot in the centre of the potato. If your potatoes are extra small, you can skip this step. The scooped out potato flesh can be discarded or set aside for another use.

BAKE THE POTATOES: Brush the potatoes inside and out with melted butter, and season with salt. Transfer to a roasting tray and bake until golden brown and crispy, 15 to 20 minutes. Let the potatoes cool slightly before filling and serving.

If making these for guests, you can do this all ahead of time and pop them under a preheated grill for a few minutes when you're ready to assemble. Let them cool slightly before filling and serving.

ASSEMBLE AND SERVE: Top each potato with crème fraîche, chives, and a dollop of caviar.

CRUSHED OLIVE SPREAD

2 cups whole or pitted green olives (I like Castelvetranos)

½ cup fresh flat-leaf parsley (thin stems are okay)

¼ cup extra-virgin olive oil

2 tablespoons capers in brine, drained and rinsed

1 garlic clove, peeled

1 small shallot, peeled

1 lemon, zested and juiced (about 2 to 3 tablespoons)

4 ounces blue cheese, freshly crumbled (about ¾ cup)

Hard crackers, for serving

Serves 4 to 6

I've converted countless olive haters to olive lovers with the introduction of my fave Castelvetrano, the meaty, mild Queen of Olives. It made me wonder what other olive experiences these haters denied themselves because of misplaced prejudices, and the first thing that came to mind was tapenade. Packed with olives, capers, and herbs, tapenade is the French answer to what belongs on bread and crackers before a meal. I've given it a dirty martini-inspired spin by pairing it with a sidecar of blue cheese. It's pretty much the perfect appetizer, regardless of your personal olive opinions.

FOR THE OLIVES: To remove the stones, smash each olive with the flat side of your knife blade. Peel the olive flesh from the stone and discard the stone.

MAKE THE TAPENADE: In a food processor, combine the olives, parsley, olive oil, capers, garlic, shallot, lemon zest, and lemon juice. Process just until the mixture is finely and uniformly chopped.

SERVE: Transfer the tapenade to a serving plate and pile the crumbled blue cheese alongside. Serve with crackers.

salads

ITALIAN CHOPPED WITH BUFFALO MOZZARELLA

For the Balsamic Vinaigrette

⅔ cup extra-virgin olive oil

⅓ cup balsamic vinegar

1 tablespoon Dijon mustard

1 tablespoon honey

1 teaspoon fresh thyme leaves

1 medium garlic clove, peeled and finely grated

¼ teaspoon kosher salt

Freshly ground black pepper

For the Salad

3 heads Little Gem lettuce, leaves separated

1 medium head radicchio (I like the Castelfranco or Chioggia varieties), leaves separated

1 cup canned cannellini or chickpeas, drained and rinsed

1 cup cherry tomatoes, halved

½ cup chopped banana peppers or pepperoncini

½ cup chopped roasted red peppers

½ cup chopped pitted Castelvetrano olives

4 ounces thinly sliced prosciutto, torn into 2-inch pieces

8 ounces buffalo mozzarella cheese, torn into 1-inch pieces

¼ cup fresh basil leaves, torn

Balsamic glaze, for serving

Flaky salt

Serves 4 to 6

We were a Friday night pizza family. And in New Jersey, if you're carrying out from your local pizza spot, then you're getting at least one order of the chopped salad. Pretty much anywhere you go, it's always the same: hunks of iceberg lettuce, some salami and ham, cubed provolone, a few stray chickpeas, and canned black olives. But with all due respect to this enduring and widely beloved salad, I always felt like it never truly reached its potential. This updated version is similar in mish-mosh spirit, but she's much more ~elevated~ and we love her for it. There's prosciutto and buffalo mozzarella, some meaty Castelvetranos, creamy white beans and roasted red peppers, and Little Gem lettuce and radicchio. It's just the thing for heaping on top of a hot fresh pizza or for dressing up for company.

MAKE THE VINAIGRETTE: In a jar with a fitted lid, combine the olive oil, vinegar, mustard, honey, thyme, garlic, salt, and a couple cracks of pepper. Shake well until emulsified.

DRESS THE LETTUCE: In a large bowl, combine the lettuce and radicchio. Drizzle over just enough dressing to coat, add a pinch of flaky salt, and toss to combine.

ASSEMBLE THE SALAD: In a serving bowl or platter layer the dressed greens with the beans, tomatoes, banana peppers, red peppers, olives, prosciutto, mozzarella, basil, and additional dressing as needed. Finish with a drizzle of balsamic glaze. Serve with extra dressing on the side.

SQUASH RIBBONS WITH PISTACHIO AND PECORINO

For the Salad

2 pounds small assorted summer squash

1 pound asparagus (the thicker, the better), tough ends trimmed

¼ cup pistachios, toasted and chopped

1 cup packed fresh basil leaves

Aged pecorino Romano or Parmesan cheese, for serving

Flaky salt and freshly ground black pepper

For the Pesto Vinaigrette

⅔ cup extra-virgin olive oil

⅓ cup Champagne vinegar or white wine vinegar

¼ cup Basil Parsley Pesto (page 144) or store-bought

¼ teaspoon kosher salt

Freshly ground black pepper

Serves 4

In culinary school, I was known for snacking on anything and everything during class—hunks of Parm, vegetable scraps, mushy mirepoix discards, raw onions, all the obvious snack choices. That constant need to graze didn't stop after school, and while on the job making lunch for a client and preparing a roasting tray's worth of veggies to throw on the barbecue, I started nibbling on the raw courgette and asparagus that had been seasoned with salt and doused in olive oil and vinegar. Not bad. *The texture was satisfyingly snappy, and I knew that with a little help from a good dressing, these veggies could go from good to great—and this salad was born.*

SLICE THE VEG: Using a mandoline, carefully slice the squash into thin ribbons. Using a vegetable peeler, carefully slice the asparagus into thin ribbons.

MAKE THE PESTO VINAIGRETTE: In a large bowl, whisk together the olive oil, vinegar, and pesto. Season with the salt and pepper to taste and set aside.

DRESS THE SALAD: Combine the sliced squash and asparagus in a large bowl with half of the pistachios. Add just enough vinaigrette to coat, a sprinkle of salt, and a couple cracks of pepper and lightly toss everything together. Gently fold in half of the basil.

PLATE & SERVE: Transfer the salad to a serving plate and drizzle with a bit more dressing. Top with the remaining pistachios, plus a sprinkle of salt and one or two cracks of pepper. Grate the pecorino directly over the plated salad and serve.

HOT TIP
Make this pesto vinaigrette the next time you make homemade pesto and put that residual pesto left behind in your food processor to good use: Just add all of the ingredients in the machine, and pulse to combine.

LOBSTER AVOCADO SALAD

For the Herb Dressing

⅔ cup mayo

¼ cup loosely packed fresh basil leaves

2 tablespoons roughly chopped fresh tarragon

2 tablespoons roughly chopped fresh chives

½ small shallot, roughly chopped

½ lemon, zested and juiced (1 to 2 tablespoons)

¼ teaspoon kosher salt

For the Salad

4 medium heirloom tomatoes, sliced ¼ inch thick

1 medium-large avocado, peeled, pitted, and sliced

1 lemon, halved

2 heads Bibb or Little Gem lettuce, leaves separated

1 head frisée lettuce or bunch of watercress, leaves separated

½ cup loosely packed fresh basil leaves, torn into 1-inch pieces

¼ cup loosely packed fresh tarragon leaves

¼ cup finely chopped fresh chives

1 pound cooked lobster meat from about 2 lobsters (page 62), cut in bite-size chunks

Extra-virgin olive oil, for drizzling

Flaky salt

Serves 4

This recipe is a celebration of summer. Juicy heirloom tomatoes, plump chunks of lobster meat, creamy avocado, tender microgreens, and a simple herb dressing to bring it all together. It pairs perfectly with a hot sunny day (or pretending it's a hot sunny day) and good company.

PREP THE DRESSING: Using a blender or immersion blender, process the mayo, basil, tarragon, chives, shallot, lemon zest, 1 tablespoon of lemon juice, and salt until smooth. Taste and adjust the seasoning, adding more salt and/or lemon juice as needed.

PREP THE VEG: Season both sides of the tomato slices with flaky salt and set aside.

Season the avocado slices with a pinch of flaky salt and a squeeze of lemon juice. Set aside.

In a large bowl, combine the Bibb lettuce, frisée, basil, and tarragon. Add a few tablespoons of dressing plus a few pinches of flaky salt and toss to coat.

ASSEMBLE AND SERVE: Arrange a layer of tomatoes and avocado over a serving platter or individual plates and drizzle them with extra-virgin olive oil, then begin to build the salad. Top the tomatoes with a pile of the lettuce mixture, layer in some of the lobster, more of the tomatoes and avocado, more lettuce, and more lobster. Finish with a sprinkle of chives, freshly grated lemon zest, and another drizzle of olive oil.

lobster tutorial

Here is an intro to cooking live lobsters at home.

STEAM THE LOBSTERS: Set a lobster steamer or steamer insert in a large stockpot. Fill the pot with 1 to 3 inches of water and bring to a boil.

While the water comes to a boil, prep the lobsters. Place the tip of a large, sharp knife in the centre of a lobster's head, then swiftly insert the knife while bringing it down to be parallel with your cutting board. This is the most humane way to kill the lobsters before cooking.

Add the lobsters to the steamer basket, cover the pot, and cook for 8 to 12 minutes, depending on the size and quantity of the lobsters that you're cooking. For 1 or 2 (1¼- to 1½-pound) lobsters, cook for 8 minutes. For 3 lobsters, cook for 10 minutes. For 4 lobsters, cook for 12 minutes. Turn off the heat and use tongs to carefully transfer the lobsters to a cutting board to cool.

BREAK DOWN THE LOBSTERS: When the lobsters are cool enough to handle, start by removing the tail, arms, and legs from the body. To do so, hold the lobster body in one hand, and the extremity in the other (see photo 1). Firmly twist in opposite directions and then pull (see photo 2). Inside of the cooked lobster you may find some green goo, called tomalley, which essentially is the liver. You can rinse this away and discard. You also may find lobster roe inside, which is reddish orange when cooked. You can rinse this away and discard, too. Set the body aside.

FOR THE TAIL MEAT, use kitchen shears to cut down the backside and/or underside of the tail. Use your hands to crack the tail open (see photo 3) and gently remove the meat.

FOR THE CLAWS, centre the base of the claw in a lobster cracker and clamp down until the shell cracks (see photo 4). Rotate the claw and crack again until you can remove the bottom half of the shell. Create an opening in the claw shell wide enough for the meat to come out in one piece. Before removing the shell meat, crack the jointed pincher of the claw (the thumb) backwards, give it a twist, then carefully remove the shell and cartilage, keeping the meat attached to the rest of the claw. Carefully wiggle out the claw meat, using a lobster fork if needed. Try keeping the claws whole for a prettier presentation.

FOR THE KNUCKLES, place each knuckle in a lobster cracker and clamp down until the shell cracks. Use your hands to open the shell wide enough for the knuckle meat to slide through in one piece, carefully using kitchen shears, if needed (see photo 5). Use a lobster fork to gently scoop out the meat.

FOR THE LEGS, remove them from the body and place on a cutting board, open side facing away from you. Place a rolling pin on the tip of the leg closest to you and roll it towards the other end while applying gentle pressure (see photo 6). This should encourage any leg meat to slide out of the shell.

FOR STORAGE: Transfer the meat to airtight containers and store in the fridge for up to 3 days.

TO REHEAT CHILLED LOBSTER MEAT: Bring a pot of water to a gentle boil. Using a slotted spoon, carefully lower the lobster pieces into the water. Simmer until warmed through but do not over cook, 60 to 90 seconds. Use the slotted spoon to remove and drain.

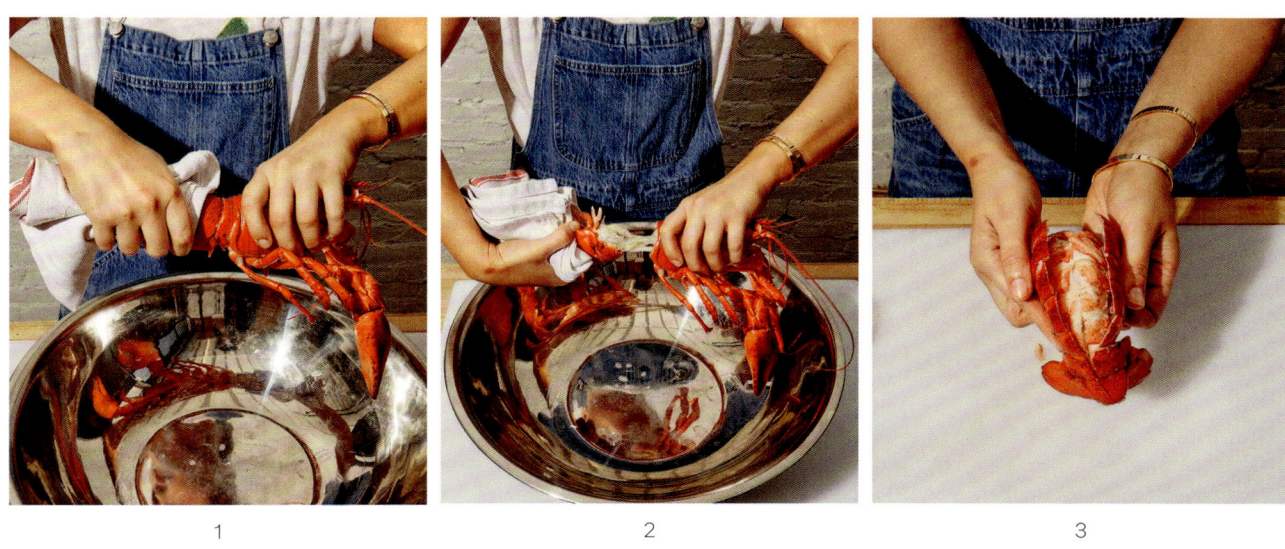

HOT TIP
I like sticking with 1¼- to 1½-pound lobsters; their meat is more tender than that from bigger lobsters. You could buy fresh lobster meat, but I strongly recommend cooking live lobsters at home. Yes, it can be a little bit of a mess, but it's going to cost you a lot less.

HOT TIP
Arguably the most delicious part of the lobster is the flavour you get from the shells. Whenever you cook lobsters at home, save the shells, make stock (take a look at the Lobster Bisque recipe, page 83), and store it in your freezer.

SALADS

THE GREEN SALAD

For the Champagne Vinaigrette

⅔ cup extra-virgin olive oil

⅓ cup Champagne vinegar or white wine vinegar

1 tablespoon Dijon mustard

1 tablespoon honey

1 teaspoon fresh thyme leaves

1 small shallot, peeled and finely chopped

½ teaspoon kosher salt

Freshly ground black pepper

For the Salad

3 heads Little Gem or Bibb lettuce, leaves separated

1 head frisée, leaves separated

Assorted microgreens or watercress

Flaky salt and freshly ground black pepper

Serves 4 full servings or 6 to 8 half servings

This is my salad blueprint inspired by the insalata verde at Via Carota. Its good sense is at the foundation of each of my salads and meets all my salad criteria: fresh, crisp greens, a high-acid dressing, and generously seasoned with flaky salt and fresh pepper. Anything beyond that is gravy. This can be served as a side salad, or made more substantial with your favourite add-ins and toppings. It's really that simple.

MAKE THE CHAMPAGNE VINAIGRETTE: In a jar with a fitted lid, combine the olive oil, vinegar, mustard, honey, thyme, shallot, salt and a couple cracks of black pepper. Seal the jar and shake until emulsified. Set aside or store in the fridge for up to 2 weeks.

MAKE THE SALAD: In a large bowl, toss together the lettuces and microgreens. Drizzle with the vinaigrette, season with additional salt and a few cracks of pepper, and gently toss to coat well. Serve piled high.

HOT TIP
To make an extra cold and crunchy salad: Wash your greens in ice water. Spin them dry, then transfer them to a kitchen towel-lined baking tray.

BLUEBERRY BBQ GRILLED CHICKEN SALAD

For the Salad

1½ pounds boneless, skinless chicken breasts

1 head butter lettuce, leaves separated and torn

4 cups mixed salad greens

1 head radicchio, leaves separated and torn

1 cup loosely packed fresh basil leaves, larger leaves torn

1 cup blueberries

4 ounces fresh goat cheese

½ cup roasted and salted sunflower seeds

Extra-virgin olive oil

Kosher salt, flaky salt, and freshly ground black pepper

For the Blueberry BBQ Sauce

½ cup Blueberry Jam (page 250) or store-bought

⅓ cup apple cider vinegar

1 teaspoon smoked red pepper flakes or crushed red pepper flakes mixed with ¼ teaspoon smoked paprika

½ teaspoon kosher salt

¼ teaspoon cayenne pepper

For the Blueberry Vinaigrette

½ cup of Blueberry Jam (page 250) or store-bought

⅓ cup apple cider vinegar

⅓ cup extra-virgin olive oil

½ small shallot, peeled and finely chopped

½ teaspoon kosher salt

Freshly ground black pepper

Serves 4 to 6

North Carolina BBQ calls for two things: pork and apple cider vinegar. We'll get to the pork later (page 210), but for now we're focusing on that one-of-a-kind vinegary barbecue sauce. My mom's steeped-in-the-South recipe uses ketchup, apple cider vinegar, and cayenne pepper, so it's tangy, a little sweet, and has a hint of spice. I've applied that formula to my "blue" BBQ sauce, which gets its sweetness from homemade blueberry jam, a flavour as quintessentially summer as standing around outside grilling chicken.

Preheat the barbecue to medium-high.

PREP THE CHICKEN: Season the chicken with kosher salt and pepper and a drizzle of olive oil. Let the chicken stand at room temperature for 10 to 20 minutes before grilling.

MAKE THE BBQ SAUCE: Using a blender or immersion blender, blend the blueberry jam, vinegar, pepper flakes, salt, and cayenne pepper until smooth. Set aside.

MAKE THE BLUEBERRY VINAIGRETTE: Using a blender or immersion blender, blend the blueberry jam, vinegar, olive oil, shallot, salt, and pepper until smooth. Set aside.

BARBECUE THE CHICKEN: Sear the chicken on both sides until good grill marks form, 3 to 5 minutes per side. Then baste the chicken in the BBQ sauce and continue grilling, turning and basting every couple of minutes, until the sauce has caramelized on the outside and the chicken reaches an internal temperature of 70°C, 4 to 6 minutes more.

Transfer the chicken to a cutting board to rest for at least 4 minutes, covering with kitchen foil to keep warm.

ASSEMBLE THE SALAD: In a large bowl, combine the butter lettuce, mixed greens, radicchio, and basil with enough vinaigrette to coat and a pinch of flaky salt. Toss to combine. Gently fold in half of the blueberries, half of the goat cheese, and half of the sunflower seeds. Transfer to a serving platter and top with the remaining blueberries, goat cheese, and sunflower seeds.

Slice the chicken into cubes and arrange it on top of the salad. Serve extra vinaigrette and BBQ sauce on the side.

CABBAGE AND HERB SALAD

Vegetable oil, for frying

6 rice paper wrappers

2 cups shredded chicken (roasted, grilled, poached, or rotisserie chicken will work)

1 medium head green cabbage, very finely shredded on a mandoline

1 medium daikon radish or 5 red radishes, julienned (see page 70)

1 large carrot, peeled and julienned (see page 70)

1 medium shallot, peeled and thinly sliced

¼ cup roasted peanuts

¼ teaspoon kosher salt

1 cup packed fresh coriander leaves

½ cup packed fresh mint leaves

Tomato Nuoc Cham (recipe follows)

½ cup store-bought crispy fried shallots or onions

Kosher salt

Serves 4

This is a love letter to one of my favourite Vietnamese dishes, gỏi gà, a salad of finely shredded cabbage, pulled chicken, fresh herbs, and fried shallots. What really makes the dish sing is the nuoc cham dressing, a sweet, salty, and slightly sour combination of fish sauce, lime juice, sugar, and garlic. I took inspiration from my favourite Brooklyn-based Vietnamese restaurant and paired this cool and crunchy salad with crispy fried rice paper, which acts as the perfect vehicle for shoveling. This salad has the main-character energy deserving of a dinner party, but it's also the kind of salad that's perfect to keep in your fridge and have all to yourself for the week.

FRY THE RICE PAPER WRAPPERS: Fill a large pot with 2 inches of the vegetable oil and heat over medium-high heat to 180°C. Set a wire rack on a roasting tray and set aside.

Cut each rice wrapper into quarters. Working in batches, drop the wrappers into the oil and fry until they're puffed up and crispy, 15 to 30 seconds. Use a slotted spoon or kitchen spider to transfer them to the wire rack to drain. Continue frying the remaining wrappers.

MAKE THE SALAD: In a large bowl, combine the chicken, cabbage, daikon, carrot, shallot, peanuts, and three-quarters of the coriander and mint. Drizzle with enough nuoc cham to coat, plus a pinch of salt and toss to combine. Plate and top with the remaining herbs, the crispy shallots, and tomatoes from the nuoc cham. Serve with crispy rice paper and additional nuoc cham.

To make the salad ahead, store each of the components in individual airtight containers in the fridge for up to 4 days.

CONTINUED

CABBAGE AND HERB SALAD

CONTINUED

TOMATO NUOC CHAM

2 cups cherry tomatoes, halved

Juice of 4 limes (about ⅓ cup)

2 tablespoons sugar

2 tablespoons fish sauce

1 Thai chilli, stemmed and finely chopped

1 medium garlic clove, peeled and finely grated

Kosher salt

Typically nuoc cham is thinned with water, but instead I opted to recruit my favourite ingredient, cherry tomatoes, to dilute the sauce with tomato water—aka the liquid released after salting them. If you want to make traditional nuoc cham, sub the tomato water with 2 additional tablespoons of hot tap water.

SALT THE TOMATOES: Put the tomatoes in a large bowl. Sprinkle with a pinch of salt and toss well. Let them stand for 10 minutes, tossing a few times. Strain through a fine-mesh sieve into a small bowl and press down to release juice from the tomatoes. Set the tomatoes aside.

MAKE THE NUOC CHAM: To the tomato water, add the lime juice, sugar, fish sauce, chilli, garlic, and 1 tablespoon very hot tap water. Stir to combine. When the sugar has dissolved, cover the bowl and place in the fridge to cool.

HOT TIP

To make extra tomato water, transfer tomatoes to a blender and blend until smooth. Set a fine-mesh sieve lined with cheesecloth over a large bowl. Transfer the mixture into the cheesecloth, cover with cling film, and transfer to the fridge to drain for 8 hours or overnight.

how to julienne

I love to julienne vegetables using the mandoline because it saves so much time and makes for much more even slices than I'd be able to do freehand (don't tell my old culinary school instructors).

First, use the mandoline to thinly slice your vegetables into uniform planks, about ⅛ inch thick or less.

Then, using a sharp knife, slice your planks into uniform matchsticks, ⅛ inch thick or less.

Always use caution when using your mandoline. They're sharp! It's best practice to use a mandoline guard or a steel glove.

BIG FAT GREEK SALAD WITH SOUVLAKI-ISH CHICKEN

For the Souvlaki-ish Chicken

2 pounds boneless, skinless chicken thighs (about 12 thighs)

¼ cup extra-virgin olive oil

1 lemon, zested and juiced (about 2 to 3 tablespoons)

2 tablespoons finely chopped fresh oregano leaves

1 medium garlic clove, peeled and grated

½ teaspoon smoked paprika

Kosher salt and freshly ground pepper

For the Salad

2 romaine hearts, finely shredded

2 mini cucumbers, halved and then thinly sliced

1 medium green bell pepper, thinly sliced

½ cup finely chopped spring onions (white and green parts, about 3 spring onions)

¼ cup roughly chopped fresh dill

10 pepperoncini peppers, stemmed and finely chopped

2 tablespoons capers in brine, drained

Extra-virgin olive oil, for serving

Red wine vinegar, for serving

½ teaspoon dried oregano

Flaky salt and freshly ground black pepper

8 ounces feta cheese (preferably in brine), crumbled

Serves 4

Inspired by maroulosalata, or Greek "lettuce salad," featuring all things green—romaine, spring onions, bell peppers, pepperoncini, capers, dill—I've given it the micro-chop treatment so every single bit makes it onto your fork. And I finish it off with juicy grilled chicken thighs that have taken a soak in a souvlaki-adjacent marinade. You could eat this as-is, or stuff it into pita bread.

MARINATE THE CHICKEN: In a large zip-top bag, combine the chicken, olive oil, lemon zest and juice, oregano, garlic, paprika, 1 teaspoon kosher salt, and a couple cracks of pepper. Seal the bag, and use your hands to ensure the chicken is well coated in the marinade. Let the chicken marinate in the fridge for at least 30 minutes or up to overnight.

BARBECUE THE CHICKEN: Remove the chicken from the fridge 30 minutes before you start cooking to allow it to come to room temperature. Preheat the barbecue to medium-high.

Remove the chicken from the bag, allowing any excess marinade to drip off. Place the thighs on the hot grill. Cook, covered and undisturbed, until the first side gets a good sear and easily releases from the grill, 8 to 10 minutes. Flip and cook, covered, until the second side is seared and the juices run clear or until the internal temp reaches 80°C, 6 to 8 minutes.

Transfer the chicken to a rimmed cutting board and cover with kitchen foil; let rest for at least 5 minutes before serving.

MAKE THE SALAD: In a large bowl, combine the romaine, cucumbers, bell pepper, spring onions, dill, pepperoncini, and capers. Drizzle with the olive oil, red wine vinegar, dried oregano, a pinch of flaky salt, and a couple cracks of black pepper and toss to combine. Gently fold in the feta, and then transfer the salad to a serving platter. Serve with the chicken thighs.

HOT TIP

For a safe and effective way to clean your barbecue, slice an onion in half and rub the onion cut side down over the hot grill grates after preheating.

PLT SALAD

For the Buttermilk Ranch

⅔ cup whole buttermilk

⅓ cup mayo

¼ cup finely chopped fresh chives

1 lemon, zested and juiced (about 2 to 3 tablespoons)

1 tablespoon finely grated shallot

1 medium garlic clove, peeled and finely grated

Kosher salt and freshly ground black pepper

For the Salad

8 ounces prosciutto

4 to 6 heads Little Gem lettuce, halved lengthwise

1 cup cherry tomatoes, halved

¼ cup chopped spring onions (white and green parts)

2 tablespoons chopped fresh chives

¼ cup Quick-Pickled Shallots (recipe follows)

2 avocados, diced

4 ounces blue cheese, freshly crumbled (about ¾ cup)

Flaky salt and freshly ground black pepper

Serves 4 to 6

QUICK-PICKLED SHALLOTS

½ cup Champagne vinegar or white wine vinegar

1 tablespoon sugar

½ teaspoon kosher salt

5 medium shallots, peeled and thinly sliced

The current zietgiest has claimed chicken Caesar salad, fries, and a Diet Coke as the ideal "adult happy meal," but let me introduce you to MY ideal adult happy meal: a wedge-adjacent salad, Kraft Mac & Cheese, and, of course, a crisp Diet Coke. Now, people often say to me, "You seem like someone who would make their own ranch dressing." And while I realize that I'm high maintenance in a lot of ways, I am still partial to a few "lowbrow" delicacies, Hidden Valley Ranch being one of them. It wasn't until I was working in a restaurant kitchen that I made the homemade stuff, and I have to say, I get it. I'm not throwing out my Hidden Valley just yet, but safe to say this is the only ranch I deem appropriate for dressing salads.

Preheat the oven to 200°C. Line a roasting tray with parchment paper.

MAKE THE BUTTERMILK RANCH: In a medium bowl, whisk together the buttermilk, mayo, chives, 1 tablespoon lemon juice, the shallot, garlic, ¼ teaspoon salt, and a couple cracks of pepper. Season with more lemon and/or salt, if needed, and set aside. The dressing can be stored in the fridge for up to 1 week.

COOK THE PROSCIUTTO: Lay the prosciutto in a single layer on the prepared roasting tray and bake until it's crisped through, 9 to 12 minutes. Transfer the prosciutto to a kitchen towel-lined plate to cool. Once cooled, break into 2-inch pieces.

ASSEMBLE THE SALAD: In a large mixing bowl, combine the lettuce and enough dressing to coat. Mix to combine. Transfer the dressed greens to a plate or a serving platter, and top with the prosciutto, tomatoes, spring onions, chives, pickled shallots, avocado, blue cheese, flaky salt, and pepper.

MAKE THE BRINE: In a medium microwave-safe container, stir together the vinegar, sugar, salt, and 1 cup of water. Microwave on high for 2 minutes and stir to dissolve the sugar.

PICKLE THE SHALLOTS: Add the shallots and let them sit for at least 15 minutes before using.

To store, transfer the shallots to an airtight container and keep in the refrigerator for up to 2 weeks.

RADICCHIO WITH HAZELNUTS AND BROWN BUTTER VINAIGRETTE

For the Brown Butter Vinaigrette

1 small shallot, peeled and finely chopped

1 teaspoon fresh thyme leaves

1 teaspoon honey

1 stick (8 tablespoons) salted butter

½ cup raw hazelnuts, roughly chopped

3 tablespoons apple cider vinegar

¼ teaspoon kosher salt

For the Salad

5 medium heads radicchio, preferably a mix of several varieties, leaves separated

6 black Mission figs, halved and/or quartered

Flaky salt and freshly ground black pepper

Serves 4 to 6

There are few things to be excited about in produce aisles during the depths of northeastern winters, but radicchio is one of the bright spots. The vibrant pink and purple hues break up the monotony of drab root vegetables, while the bitter bite pairs perfectly with rich and indulgent winter flavours, in this case brown butter.

TOAST THE HAZELNUTS AND MAKE THE VINAIGRETTE: In a medium heatproof bowl, combine the shallot, thyme, and honey. Set a fine-mesh sieve over the top and set aside.

Melt the butter in a medium pan over medium-low heat. Cook, stirring occasionally, until it begins to foam, about 5 minutes. Add the hazelnuts and continue cooking and stirring until the butter browns, about 2 minutes more.

Strain the brown butter through the sieve into the bowl with the shallot, thyme, and honey. Transfer the toasted hazelnuts to a plate to cool. Whisk the shallot mixture until the honey is dissolved, then whisk in the vinegar and salt.

ASSEMBLE THE SALAD: Place the radicchio in a large bowl and drizzle with enough vinaigrette to coat. Add a sprinkle of flaky salt and a few cracks of black pepper and toss to coat.

To serve, layer half of the radicchio on a serving platter. Scatter with some of the figs and hazelnuts and repeat the layering. Spoon over extra dressing and serve the rest on the side.

HOT TIP
You'll want to serve this right away because the butter in the dressing will solidify as it cools. If you prep the dressing ahead of time, just reheat it in the microwave for 15 to 30 seconds until the butter melts. The dressing can be stored in the fridge in a tightly covered container for up to 1 week.

soups

RIBOLLITA

1 large yellow onion, peeled and roughly chopped

3 celery stalks, finely chopped

1 large carrot, peeled and finely chopped

2 medium garlic cloves, peeled and crushed

2 tablespoons tomato paste

1 cup dry white wine, such as Pinot Grigio

4 cups chicken or vegetable stock

2 (14-ounce) cans whole peeled tomatoes

1 tablespoon fresh thyme leaves

1 tablespoon chopped Calabrian chillies, or more or less to taste

1 Parmesan cheese rind (optional)

½ sourdough boule, torn into 1- to 2-inch pieces

1 (14-ounce) can cannellini beans, drained and rinsed

1 large bunch Tuscan kale, leaves stripped and roughly torn (about 5 cups)

2 ounces freshly grated Parmesan cheese (about ½ cup)

Extra-virgin olive oil

Kosher salt and freshly ground black pepper

Serves 4 to 6

My rendition of this traditional and rustic Italian soup is anything but traditional and rustic. A little trick I picked up during my private chef years is the magic of an immersion blender (as I'm sure you've picked up on), and this soup is the perfect example of its powers. What would normally be a pot of diced veg and beans suspended in broth is transformed into a luscious and silky soup that will send your eyes rolling into the back of your head. If that's not reason enough to add an immersion blender to your kitchen tool kit, IDK what is.

Preheat the oven to 200°C.

MAKE THE SOUP BASE: Heat a large cast-iron casserole dish over medium-high heat and add ¼ cup of olive oil. When the oil shimmers, add the onion, celery, carrot, garlic, tomato paste, ¼ teaspoon of salt, and a few cracks of pepper. Cook, stirring occasionally, until the vegetables start to soften and the tomato paste has caramelized, 7 to 10 minutes.

Pour in the wine, stirring with a wooden spoon to scrape up any brown bits from the bottom of the pot. Cook until the wine reduces by about two-thirds, 5 minutes. Add the stock, tomatoes, thyme, Calabrian chillies, and Parm rind (if using). Bring the soup to a low boil, then reduce to a simmer and cook, stirring occasionally, until the vegetables are tender, 30 minutes.

MAKE THE CROUTONS: Put the torn sourdough in a large bowl and toss with 2 tablespoons olive oil and ¼ teaspoon salt. On a roasting tray, spread the bread in a single layer. Bake until the bread is golden brown, 15 to 20 minutes, flipping the pieces halfway through. Set aside to cool.

BLEND AND ASSEMBLE THE SOUP: Turn off the heat and remove and discard the Parm rind. Use an immersion blender to blend the soup until smooth. Alternatively, you could do this in batches in a blender, but be sure to allow the soup to cool before doing so.

Turn the heat back to medium-high, add the beans, and simmer for another 5 minutes. Fold in the kale and cook just long enough for it to wilt but not go soggy, 3 to 5 minutes. Remove the pot from the heat and cover to keep warm until ready to serve.

SERVE: Ladle the soup into bowls, top with a drizzle of olive oil, a generous sprinkle of Parm, and a pile of toasted croutons.

LOBSTER BISQUE

2 (1½-pound) live lobsters

1 stick plus 2 tablespoons (10 tablespoons) salted butter

3 medium carrots, chopped

3 celery stalks, chopped

1 small yellow onion, peeled and chopped

1 small fennel bulb, chopped

1 small leek, chopped

6 garlic cloves, smashed and peeled

¼ cup tomato paste

1 cup dry sherry

2 quarts good fish stock (see Hot Tip), or Shrimp Stock (page 166)

¼ cup double cream (optional but encouraged)

¼ cup chopped fresh chives

Kosher salt

Serves 4 to 6

To say that my family is obsessed with lobster bisque is a massive understatement. We've had this creamy, lobster-chunked soup every year for Christmas Eve for as long as I can remember, and every year my mom would drive 2 hours roundtrip to the Jersey Shore to get the very best one. So I figured if I could make a version that's worth four hours in the car, then I could save her the soup road trip—and the 30 bucks a quart. Spoiler alert: I did it. The trick, I found, was relying not on the usual suspects to thicken the broth (rice, roux, and/or a boatload of cream), but instead starting with homemade lobster stock, and then pureeing the veg from the stock for a luscious and creamy consistency: cream not required. Oh, and because we're making it for ourselves, we can load it up with as much lobster as we like, which is entirely the point.

PREP THE LOBSTERS: Steam the lobsters according to the directions on page 62 and remove the meat from the shells (see page 63), reserving the shells for the stock. Clean the lobster bodies by breaking them open and removing the gills and eyeballs so just the shell remains. Discard any small broken pieces of shell to avoid having to hand pick them out of the stock later.

MAKE THE STOCK: Heat a large cast-iron casserole dish over medium heat and melt 8 tablespoons of the butter. Add the lobster shells and cook, stirring a few times, until lightly toasted and fragrant, about 5 minutes.

Add the carrots, celery, onion, fennel, leek, and garlic. Season with a pinch of salt and cook until the vegetables have softened, about 5 minutes. Stir in the tomato paste and cook until it is browned and caramelized, about 4 minutes. Pour in the sherry and use a wooden spoon to stir and scrape up any brown bits from the bottom of the pot. Let the sherry simmer until it reduces by about half, about 5 minutes.

Add about 2 quarts of fish stock and bring to a boil. Reduce the heat to low and simmer the stock, uncovered, until it has a rich lobster taste, 60 to 90 minutes. Turn off the heat and cool the stock before straining.

CONTINUED

LOBSTER BISQUE

CONTINUED

STRAIN THE STOCK through a large fine-mesh sieve and set the liquid aside. Pick out all of the shells and discard, reserving the veg.

Transfer the veg back to the pot along with 3 cups of the strained stock and blend with an immersion blender until smooth. We want to achieve a consistency thick enough to coat the back of a spoon, but not so thick that it resembles more of a puree than a soup. If the soup is too thick, add more stock, a little at a time. If the soup is too thin, bring to a simmer reduce until thickened.

If preparing in advance, transfer the bisque and cooked lobster meat into separate airtight containers and store in the fridge for up to 3 days. I don't recommend freezing the lobster meat, but you can freeze the bisque and any leftover lobster stock for up to 6 months.

ASSEMBLE THE BISQUE: Bring the bisque to a simmer over medium heat. Stir in the cream (if using) and season with salt to taste. Add half of the chopped lobster meat, setting aside the prettiest pieces for garnish, and simmer just until the soup is warmed through, about 5 minutes.

PREP THE LOBSTER GARNISH: Reheat the lobster meat according to the directions on page 62. Heat a small saucepan over medium heat and add the remaining 2 tablespoons of butter. When the butter begins to bubble, turn off the heat and add the warm lobster meat. Swirl the pieces in the butter and add a sprinkle of chives.

SERVE: Ladle the soup into wide bowls. Portion the buttered lobster pieces into each bowl, drizzling any remaining butter from the pan over top. Finish with a sprinkle of chives.

HOT TIP
Starting your lobster stock with fish stock will make for an extra flavoursome broth. This process is what we call "fortifying a stock" in the culinary world. Pick up some fresh or frozen fish stock at the fish store, or I like the brand Aneto for boxed fish stock. Be sure to taste it before using to make sure you like it. And if you can't find a good fish stock, you can sub with the Shrimp Stock from page 166—or you can also just use water, but if you do, simmer the stock for an additional 2 hours (3 hours total).

HOT TIP
You can easily make this normally dairy-heavy dish dairy-free by swapping the butter for olive oil and skipping the double cream.

GREEN GARLIC AND GINGER CHICKEN SOUP

4 cups chicken stock, broth, or bone broth

4 cups packed fresh baby spinach

1 heaping cup cooked short-grain rice

1 cup packed fresh flat-leaf parsley leaves, plus more for garnish

2 stalks green garlic or 2 spring onions

2 to 3 medium jalapeños (depending on your heat preference), plus sliced jalapeños for garnish

4 medium garlic cloves, peeled

1 (2-inch) knob fresh ginger, peeled and grated

1 cup cooked and pulled chicken, from leftover roast chicken or rotisserie

Soy sauce

2 lemons or limes, cut into wedges, for serving

Kosher salt

Serves 4 to 6

This green swampy slop, lovingly referred to as Swamp Soup, started as my go-to sick day soup, but my cravings for it sustained even after cold and flu season ended. Packed with ginger, garlic, and spinach, its bold, spicy punch of flavour makes it feel like anything but medicine. Another strong selling point for the soup is its ability to be prepared in large quantities and stored in the freezer for when the next sick day strikes.

WILT THE SPINACH: In a large cast-iron casserole dish or pot, bring the chicken stock to a boil. Stir in the spinach and cook just until it wilts, about 1 minute. Use a slotted spoon to transfer the spinach to a blender and set aside to cool. (Do not ignore the cooling step; blending hot things can cause your blender to explode.)

Add the rice to the broth and allow the liquid to return to a boil. Lower the heat and simmer, uncovered, until the liquid has thickened and the rice begins to break apart, 10 to 15 minutes. Turn off the heat when the desired consistency is reached.

MAKE THE GREEN GARLIC AND GINGER PUREE: Add the parsley, green garlic, whole jalapeños, garlic, ginger, 1 teaspoon of salt, and ¼ cup water to the cooled spinach. Blend until smooth, about 60 seconds. If the mixture gets stuck, add a splash more water.

ASSEMBLE: Fold the chicken into the rice-thickened broth along with about half of the garlic-and-ginger puree. Taste and add a bit more puree until the soup is flavoured to your liking. I go full-batch puree, but not everyone loves how pungent it can be. Season with more salt and a few splashes of soy sauce to taste and turn off the heat.

SERVE: Ladle the soup into bowls and finish with parsley and a few jalapeño slices. Serve with a wedge of lemon or lime.

Store leftovers in an airtight container in the fridge for up to 4 days or in the freezer for up to 6 months.

HOT TIP
I leave the garlic, ginger, and jalapeño raw so their immune-boosting, Vitamin C-packed benefits are at max force. However, if you are prone to heartburn, sauté them for a few minutes before blending.

CHICKEN KHAO SOI

For the Khao Soi Paste

⅓ cup coriander stems

8 large garlic cloves, peeled

2 medium shallots, peeled

2 Thai chillies, or 1 red Fresno chilli

1 (2-inch) knob fresh ginger, peeled

2 tablespoons crushed red pepper flakes

2 teaspoons ground turmeric

2 teaspoons ground coriander

2 teaspoons curry powder

For the Soup

4 bone-in, skin-on chicken legs

1 tablespoon coconut oil or vegetable oil

4 cups chicken stock

1 (14-ounce) can full-fat coconut milk

3 tablespoons fish sauce, plus more as needed

2 teaspoons light brown sugar

Cooked egg noodles, for serving

Quick-Pickled Shallots (page 74)

Fresh coriander leaves

2 limes, sliced into wedges

Kosher salt

Serves 4 to 6

This dish was the gateway to my obsession with Southeast Asian flavours. It's spicy, gingery, bright, punchy, and oh-so-cosy and comforting. Khao Soi is a curry noodle soup with roots in Northern Thailand, Laos, and Myanmar. The base starts with a homemade curry paste and coconut milk for a complex and creamy broth. Chicken is then braised in the broth until falling-apart tender, and ladled over satisfyingly chewy egg noodles. Typically, it's topped with thinly sliced shallots, coriander, lime wedges, pickled mustard greens, and crispy fried noodles. I've adapted this version to be made using ingredients more readily available in grocery stores, by swapping the pickled mustard greens for pickled shallots and the fried noodles for crispy chicken skin.

Preheat the oven to 220°C.

MAKE THE KHAO SOI PASTE: In a food processor, combine the coriander stems, garlic, shallots, chillies, ginger, red pepper flakes, turmeric, coriander, and curry powder. Pulse until the mixture forms a smooth paste.

MAKE THE SOUP: Remove the skin from the chicken and set it aside. Season the chicken all over with salt.

Heat a large cast-iron casserole dish over medium heat and add the oil. When the oil shimmers, add the curry paste and cook, stirring, until it begins to stick to the pan, about 3 minutes. Whisk in the stock, coconut milk, and a pinch of salt.

Add the chicken and allow the mixture to come to a boil. Reduce to a gentle simmer and cook, partially covered, until the meat is falling-off-the-bone tender, about 1 hour. Turn off the heat and stir in the fish sauce and brown sugar. Season with more fish sauce or salt, if needed.

WHILE THE CHICKEN SIMMERS, MAKE THE CRISPY SKIN: Line a roasting tray with kitchen foil and a wire rack. Pat the chicken skin dry with a kitchen towel and lay it on the prepared roasting tray. Bake until golden and crispy, flipping halfway through, about 20 minutes. Set aside to cool.

SERVE: Fill each bowl with noodles and top with the chicken (shredded or whole, up to you). Ladle over the broth and finish with the pickled shallots, coriander, and crispy chicken skin. Serve with lime wedges.

sammies

ULTIMATE ITALIAN

2 red bell peppers or
1 (16-ounce) jar roasted red peppers, chopped

1 loaf focaccia bread, about 10 inches round, or
a 9 x 10-inch rectangle

5 cups packed baby rocket

Balsamic vinegar

1 cup Basil Parsley Pesto (page 144) or store-bought

8 ounces thinly sliced prosciutto

8 ounces thinly sliced mortadella

12 ounces stracciatella cheese, store-bought or homemade (page 35), or burrata cheese

Flaky salt and freshly ground black pepper

Extra-virgin olive oil

Serves 6

This is your big Italian sub, reimagined. It's all the same basic components that make it what it is—cured meat + cheese + olive oil + balsamic—but taken to a slightly more elevated place. We're swapping salami and ham for prosciutto and mortadella, provolone for stracciatella, adding roasted red peppers and peppery rocket, and piling it all on top of one big round of focaccia. Serve this at your next Super Bowl party; bring it to the beach; or scale it down and make a sandwich for one.

Preheat the oven to 200°C.

ROAST THE RED PEPPERS: Turn on two burners of a gas stove. Rest each pepper on the burner grates above the open flames. Cook until the entire exterior is charred, using tongs to turn the peppers every 30 seconds or so. Transfer the charred peppers to a heatproof bowl and cover tightly with cling film. Let the peppers steam for about 20 minutes. Use a clean tea towel to rub away the charred skin. Most of it will slip off; it's fine if some charred spots remain. Remove the stems and seeds and roughly chop.

PREP THE BREAD: Use a serrated knife to carefully slice the focaccia in half like a big hamburger bun. Place each half of the bread, cut side down, directly on the oven racks to lightly toast, 5 to 7 minutes.

ASSEMBLE AND SERVE: In a large bowl, toss together the rocket, a pinch of flaky salt, and a drizzle of olive oil and balsamic vinegar.

Spread the pesto over both sides of the toasted focaccia. Layer the prosciutto, mortadella, and roasted red peppers on the bottom half. Dollop the stracciatella over the top, drizzle with olive oil and balsamic and add a pinch of flaky salt and a crack or two of pepper. Pile on the dressed rocket and top with focaccia. Use a sharp serrated knife to slice the sub into smaller portions and serve.

HOT BUTTERED LOBSTER ROLLS

1 pound cooked lobster meat, or the meat from 2 (1½-pound) steamed lobsters (see page 62)

2 tablespoons mayo

4 split-top buns

4 tablespoons clarified butter or ghee

2 tablespoons finely chopped fresh chives

2 tablespoons loosely packed fresh tarragon

2 tablespoons finely chopped Quick-Pickled Shallots (page 74)

Kosher salt

1 head Bibb lettuce, leaves separated

1 lemon, sliced into wedges

Makes 4 rolls

There are two camps when it comes to lobster rolls: Maine style and Connecticut style. Growing up, I was only exposed to the Maine-style rolls with cold lobster meat suspended in mayo, served on a hot dog bun. I found them underwhelming at best, but I played along. It wasn't until my early twenties when I discovered the Connecticut alternative: large chunks of lobster meat bathed in hot butter and nestled in a toasted brioche bun. I haven't looked back since. And it truly pains me to think of how many others have suffered in silence without the joy of a proper lobster roll experience.

Preheat the oven to 90°C.

PREP THE LOBSTER: Chop your lobster meat into 1- to 2-inch pieces, leaving the claws intact for presentation. If using freshly cooked lobster, cover to keep warm.

TOAST THE BUNS: Heat a large saucepan or frying pan over medium-low heat. Spread a layer of mayo on the sides of the buns. Working in batches, add the buns to the saucepan, mayo side down. Toast both sides until golden brown, 1 to 2 minutes per side. Keep the buns warm in the oven for up to 15 minutes.

HEAT AND BUTTER THE LOBSTER: If using pre-cooked lobster meat that is cold from the fridge, follow the reheating instructions on page 62. If using freshly cooked lobster meat that is still warm, you can skip this step.

Add the butter to a pan and heat over medium-low heat until melted and bubbling. Add the lobster meat and toss to coat in the butter.

Turn off the heat and add the chives and tarragon, pickled shallots, and a pinch of salt. Toss to combine. Cover with a lid while you assemble the lobster rolls.

ASSEMBLE AND SERVE: Arrange the warm buns cut side up on a serving tray and line each with lettuce. Immediately divide the warm lobster meat among the buns and serve right away with lemon wedges.

CHICKEN CUTLET CLUB

1½ pounds boneless, skinless chicken breasts, sliced and pounded into ¼-inch-thick cutlets

½ cup plain flour

2 medium eggs, beaten

2 cups panko bread crumbs

8 slices bacon

Vegetable oil, for frying

12 slices soft white sandwich bread

2 medium ripe tomatoes, preferably heirloom, sliced ¼ inch thick

½ medium head green cabbage, very finely shredded on a mandoline (about 3 cups)

1 cup Buttermilk Ranch (page 74)

Kosher salt and freshly ground black pepper

Makes 4 sandwiches

I love a club sandwich, and I feel a personal obligation to order it whenever it's on a menu. So I wanted to create a version catering to my own, very niche, personal preferences, because isn't that what recipe developing is all about? My ideal club sandwich contains a ranch-y panko fried cutlet (that's not too thin but not too thick), oven-cooked bacon, very finely shaved cabbage, salted heirloom tomatoes, all drenched in homemade ranch.

Preheat the oven to 200°C.

BREAD THE CUTLETS: Set up a dredging station with separate wide, shallow bowls for the flour, the eggs, and the panko. Season the chicken with salt and pepper. Working with one cutlet at a time, coat each one in flour, then egg wash, then panko, pressing the crumbs in so they adhere. Transfer the breaded cutlets to a roasting tray or a plate and into the fridge for 15 minutes for the breading to set.

COOK THE BACON: Arrange the bacon in a single layer on a foil-lined rimmed baking sheet and bake until crispy, about 15 to 20 minutes for thick cut. Transfer to a kitchen towel-lined plate to drain and cool.

FRY THE CUTLETS: Add 1 to 2 inches of oil to a high-sided pan. Heat over medium-high heat until the oil reaches 180°C. Test the oil temperature by dropping in a few panko crumbs; they should sizzle immediately but not burn. Fry the cutlets, working in batches, until golden brown, about 3 minutes per side. Transfer the cooked chicken to a wire rack-lined roasting tray to let the excess oil drain and season with a pinch of salt.

TOAST THE BREAD AND PREP THE VEG: Lightly toast each slice of bread in a toaster until barely golden. Season the sliced tomatoes with salt and pepper and transfer to a kitchen towel-lined plate to absorb excess moisture. In a large mixing bowl, combine the cabbage with enough ranch to coat and a pinch of salt. Toss to combine.

ASSEMBLE AND SERVE: To build each sandwich, start with a slice of toasted bread and layer on a handful of dressed cabbage, a fried cutlet, a hefty drizzle of ranch dressing, a second slice of bread, 2 pieces of bacon, 1 to 2 slices of tomato, another handful of cabbage, more ranch to taste, and a final piece of bread.

Skewer with toothpicks in each of the four corners, then use a sharp serrated knife to cut each sandwich into quarters. Serve with extra ranch for dipping.

GREEN CURRY KATSU SANDO

For the Green Curry Sauce

1 cup full-fat coconut milk

1 cup packed fresh baby spinach

½ cup loosely packed fresh coriander leaves and stems

1 teaspoon Thai green curry paste

½ small shallot, peeled and roughly chopped

1 (½-inch) knob ginger, peeled and roughly chopped

1 teaspoon fish sauce

½ teaspoon sugar

1 lime, zested

¼ teaspoon kosher salt

For the Sandos

1 cup plain flour

2 medium eggs, beaten

2 cups panko bread crumbs

4 flounder fillets, about 4 to 6 ounces each

Vegetable oil, for frying

8 slices of Japanese milk bread or any soft white sandwich bread

Kewpie mayo, optional

½ small head green cabbage, very finely shredded on a mandoline (about 2 cups)

2 limes, sliced into wedges

Kosher salt and freshly ground black pepper

Makes 4 sandwiches

I dreamt up this recipe combination by combining my favourite components of various different dishes. I wondered: What if a Japanese katsu curry, typically prepared with a golden curry sauce, was swapped with a Thai green curry sauce? And what if that was then repackaged into a Japanese katsu sando? And what if the katsu was a fillet of fish? And thus, the Green Curry Katsu Sando was born. Now, if fried fish sandwiches aren't exactly your thing, I'm begging you to try this one. If you're still not convinced, feel free to swap with the protein of your choice.

MAKE THE SAUCE: In a blender, combine the coconut milk, spinach, coriander, curry paste, shallot, ginger, fish sauce, sugar, lime zest, and salt and blend until smooth.

BREAD THE FILLETS: Set up a dredging station with separate wide, shallow bowls for the flour, the eggs, and the panko. Season the fillets with salt and pepper. Working with one fillet at a time, coat each one in flour, then egg wash, then panko, pressing the crumbs in so they adhere. Transfer the breaded fillets to a roasting tray or a plate and into the fridge for 15 minutes for the breading to set.

FRY THE FILLETS: Add 1 to 2 inches of oil to a high-sided pan. Heat over medium-high heat until the oil reaches 180°C. Test the oil temperature by dropping in a few panko crumbs; they should sizzle immediately but not burn. Fry the fillets, working in batches, until golden brown, about 2 minutes per side. Transfer the cooked fillets to a wire rack-lined roasting tray to let the excess oil drain, and season with a pinch of salt.

ASSEMBLE THE SANDWICHES: Spread a thin layer of mayo (if using) on each slice of bread. Add a fillet to a slice of bread and spoon over some curry sauce. Top with shredded cabbage, a squeeze of lime juice, and then the second slice of bread. Use a serrated knife to carefully slice the sandwich in half. Serve with additional curry sauce and lime wedges.

PIRI-PIRI CHICKEN SANDWICHES

For the Piri-Piri chicken

1 medium red bell pepper

1 medium jalapeño

½ cup extra-virgin olive oil, plus more as needed

8 medium garlic cloves, smashed and peeled

3 dried piri-piri peppers, or 1 teaspoon crushed red pepper flakes

½ cup packed fresh coriander leaves

½ cup packed fresh flat-leaf parsley leaves

Juice of 1 lemon (2 to 3 tablespoons)

2 teaspoons smoked paprika

½ teaspoon granulated sugar

¼ teaspoon cayenne pepper, or more for extra spice

2 pounds boneless, skinless chicken thighs (8 to 12 thighs, depending on their size)

Kosher salt and freshly ground black pepper

For the Sandwiches

4 cups packed baby rocket

1 lemon, sliced into wedges

Flaky salt

Brioche buns or any slightly sweet sandwich rolls

Quick-Pickled Shallots (page 74)

Makes 4 to 6 sandwiches

When I fall for a dish, I fall hard, and the chicken sandwich from Nando's PERi PERi Chicken is on that list. The obsession is so severe that I would plan my entire thirteen-hour drive to and from college around a stop in Washington, DC, just for this sandwich. The star is the piri-piri sauce, named for the piri-piri peppers of which it's made. The peppers, and this dish, are native to South Africa but were imported to Portugal, leaving ties in both countries. It's garlicky and spicy, and it yields an unbelievably juicy chicken.

Preheat the barbecue to high.

MAKE THE SAUCE: Coat the bell pepper and jalapeño in olive oil. Transfer to the grill and cook, turning every few minutes, until completely charred on the outside, 8 to 10 minutes. Turn off the grill.

Transfer the peppers to a bowl and cover tightly with cling film. Allow them to steam and cool slightly, about 20 minutes. Remove the skins and stems of both peppers. Remove the seeds of the bell pepper, but leave them intact in the jalapeño for the heat.

In a food processor, combine the roasted peppers with the ½ cup olive oil, the garlic, piri-piri peppers, coriander, parsley, lemon juice, paprika, sugar, cayenne pepper, and 1 teaspoon salt. Process until smooth.

MARINATE THE CHICKEN: Place the chicken in a large zip-top bag along with half of the sauce. Marinate in the refrigerator for at least 2 hours or ideally overnight. Store the remaining marinade in a sealed container in the fridge.

COOK THE CHICKEN: Preheat the barbecue to medium-high. Remove the chicken from the marinade and allow any excess to drip off. Discard the marinade.

Grill the chicken until caramelized on the outside and the internal temp reaches 80°C, about 7 minutes per side. During the final few minutes of cooking, baste the chicken with some of the reserved sauce.

ASSEMBLE AND SERVE: In a large bowl, toss together the rocket, a squeeze of lemon juice, and a pinch of flaky salt.

Add 1 or 2 chicken thighs to each bun and top with more sauce, pickled shallots, and rocket. Serve with a lemon wedge and additional sauce on the side.

PORK SAUSAGE BURGERS

2 pounds pork mince

½ cup chopped fresh flat-leaf parsley leaves

3 tablespoons chopped Calabrian chillies, plus more to taste

4 medium garlic cloves, peeled and finely grated

1½ teaspoons whole fennel seeds, coarsely crushed with a mortar and pestle

1½ teaspoons dried oregano

3 medium bell peppers, assorted colours, stemmed, seeded, and thinly sliced

1 medium yellow onion, peeled and thinly sliced

½ cup Lemon Aïoli (page 43) or mayo, for serving

1 medium fennel bulb, very thinly sliced

1 lemon, halved

6 slices provolone cheese

6 Italian semolina rolls

Extra-virgin olive oil

Kosher salt and freshly ground black pepper

Makes 6 burgers

This is my homage to sausage and peppers, my go-to order at Yankees games, reimagined into a burger. A homemade pork sausage patty gets all dressed up with a slathering of lemon aïoli spiked with Calabrian chillies, plus jammy peppers and onions, and a crisp and crunchy fennel and parsley slaw.

Preheat the oven to 200°C.

PREP THE BURGERS: In a large bowl, combine the pork, ¼ cup of the parsley, 2 tablespoons of the Calabrian chillies, the garlic, fennel seeds, oregano, and 1 teaspoon salt. Use your hands to gently mix everything until well incorporated. Don't overmix or your burgers will get tough.

Divide the mixture into 6 equal portions and gently form them into ½-inch-thick patties. Place the patties on a roasting tray and chill in the fridge for at least 30 minutes.

ROAST THE PEPPERS AND ONIONS: In a large bowl, toss together the bell peppers and onion with about 1½ tablespoons of olive oil plus 1 teaspoon salt and a couple cracks of pepper. Transfer the veg to a large roasting tray and roast, tossing halfway through, until softened and caramelized, about 40 minutes.

PREP THE TOPPINGS: In a small bowl, whisk together the lemon aïoli and the remaining 1 tablespoon of Calabrian chillies.

In a large bowl, toss together the fennel, remaining ¼ cup of parsley, a squeeze of lemon juice, a pinch of salt, and a couple cracks of pepper. Set aside.

GRILL THE BURGERS AND BUNS: Preheat a barbecue to medium-high 10 minutes before grilling. Cook the burgers for about 5 minutes per side, topping with a slice of cheese during the last few minutes. Transfer to a plate or cutting board and loosely cover with kitchen foil. While the burgers cook, toast the buns, cut side down, until just barely warmed through, 1 to 2 minutes. Set aside.

ASSEMBLE AND SERVE: Spread the aïoli over both halves of each roll. On the bottom buns, layer the peppers and onions, a burger, fennel slaw, and a top bun.

STEAK "TARTARE" SANDWICH

For the Tartare Sauce

2 medium egg yolks

2 tablespoon capers in brine, drained and roughly chopped

2 tablespoons finely chopped gherkin pickles, plus whole pickles for serving

2 tablespoons Dijon mustard

1 small shallot, peeled and finely chopped

¼ cup extra-virgin olive oil

1 tablespoon Champagne vinegar

2 tablespoons finely chopped fresh flat-leaf parsley leaves

Kosher salt and freshly ground black pepper

For the Sandwiches

1½ pounds hanger steak or skirt steak

1 large French baguette, sliced in half lengthwise and portioned into 6-inch pieces

Good-quality salted butter, at room temperature

4 cups packed baby rocket

Flaky salt and freshly ground pepper

Makes 4 sandwiches

Steak tartare is one of my favourite foods, but raw beef isn't always the vibe people want for dinner (understandably). So I've taken all of the token flavours of steak tartare—capers, gherkins, shallots, Dijon, and parsley—and whisked them into what I'm calling a ~tartare sauce~. See what I did there? The heavenly sauce is then spooned over medium-rare steak and sandwiched between slices of toasted and buttered baguette. A combination so diabolically divine, even a Frenchman would approve (maybe).

Preheat the grill to medium-high.

MAKE THE SAUCE: In a medium bowl, whisk together the egg yolks, capers, gherkins, mustard, shallot, a pinch of salt, and a couple cracks of pepper. Continue whisking as you slowly stream in the olive oil, until the mixture emulsifies, then whisk in the vinegar and parsley. Taste and season with more salt, if needed.

COOK THE STEAK AND TOAST THE BREAD: Liberally season both sides of the meat with salt and pepper. Grill the steak until it is charred on the outside and has reached an internal temperature of 50°C, about 4 minutes per side. Let the steak rest for 5 minutes before slicing.

Add the bread to the grill, cut side down, and grill until toasted, about 2 minutes.

ASSEMBLE AND SERVE: Thinly slice the steak on a diagonal against the grain and season with flaky salt. Spread a layer of butter on all the cut sides of the bread. On the 4 bottom pieces of bread add some steak, a generous drizzle of the tartare sauce, and rocket and top with the other pieces of bread. Serve with extra gherkins.

veg

BLANCHED SPRING VEG

1 pound green vegetables, such as green beans, sugar snap peas, asparagus, broccoli

2 tablespoons extra-virgin olive oil

1 lemon, zested and halved

Kosher salt and flaky salt

Suggested Cook Times for Stand-Out Blanched Veg Options

Broccoli florets, Tenderstem broccoli, or broccoli rabe: 2 to 3 minutes

Green beans: 3 to 5 minutes

Asparagus: 2 to 4 minutes

Sugar snap peas or mange tout: 1 to 2 minutes

I am starting off the veg chapter with three key veg-cooking techniques. Part 1 takes on blanching. When I make vegetables for myself at home, nine times out of ten, I blanch them. To me it's as simple as boiling pasta.

My rule of thumb with most veg, but especially blanched veg, is that you need to dress them like you would salad greens: with salt, fat, and acid. I like flaky salt because it adds texture. For fat, my go-tos are a drizzle of really good extra-virgin olive oil, chilli-infused olive oil, or butter. Then for acid, I like lemon zest and juice or a drizzle of vinegar. If you have some salad dressing on hand (like the Lemon Vinaigrette on page 111), that works, too.

BLANCH THE VEG: In a large pot, bring 5 quarts of water to a boil and add 1 tablespoon kosher salt. While the water comes to a boil, prep an ice bath by adding a couple handfuls of ice to a large bowl and filling it with cold water. Add the veg to the boiling water and cook (see left for suggested cook times). Use a slotted spoon to transfer the veg to the ice bath until they're completely cool and then drain and pat dry.

ASSEMBLE AND SERVE: Transfer to a bowl and season with olive oil, flaky salt, lemon zest, and a squeeze of lemon juice. Toss to coat. Plate and serve.

HOT TIP

You don't technically have to shock the veg in an ice bath. As someone who has lived the past decade of her life without an ice maker, I know cubes are sacred and I wouldn't waste them on weeknight broccoli. However, if you're making these for a dinner party and want them to retain their bright green colour, shocking them in an ice bath is totally worth it.

GRILLED SUMMER VEG

For the Lemon Vinaigrette

½ cup extra-virgin olive oil

1 small shallot, peeled and finely chopped

1 lemon, zested and juiced (about 2 to 3 tablespoons)

1 tablespoon Dijon mustard

1 tablespoon honey

¼ teaspoon kosher salt

Freshly ground black pepper

For the Veg

Assorted summer squash, halved lengthwise

Assorted summer peppers, quartered

Medium-large summer tomatoes, halved or quartered

Sicilian aubergine or baby aubergine, halved lengthwise

Small sweet onions, peeled and quartered

Extra-virgin olive oil

1 lemon, zested

Fresh herbs, such as basil, parsley, or tarragon

Kosher salt and flaky salt

Part 2 of key veg-cooking techniques is barbecueing. I've barbecueed A LOT of vegetables during my four summers of private cheffing in the Hamptons. Key to a good batch of barbecued veggies is to slightly undercook then finish them with a perfectly tart vinaigrette. This is another no-recipe recipe in that it lacks definitive measurements and strict instructions. (This is how I'd write all of my recipes, if I could). I encourage you to go to a local farmers market and grab an assortment of whatever produce looks good, about ½ pound per person/serving. Cut the selections into semi-uniform-size pieces, season with olive oil, salt, and pepper, and throw them on a hot barbecue just until grill marks appear. Splash with vinaigrette and fresh herbs and call it a day.

MAKE THE VINAIGRETTE: In a jar with a fitted lid, combine the olive oil, shallot, lemon zest and juice, mustard, honey, salt, and a couple cracks of pepper. Cover, shake until emulsified, and set aside.

PREP THE VEG: Preheat the barbecue or grill to medium-high.

Your veg should be cut into 3- to 4-inch pieces, keeping them large enough that they don't fall through the grill grates. For smaller veg, such as pattypan squash and cherry tomatoes, use a grill basket or wire rack.

Spread the selections over one to two roasting trays and drizzle with enough olive oil to coat plus about ½ teaspoon of salt per pound of veg.

GRILL THE VEG: Working in batches, transfer the veg to the hot barbecue or grill. Cook until the veg are charred yet still tender, turning occasionally. Timing varies depending on the size of veg and the heat from your barbecue or grill, 4 to 10 minutes. The veg will continue cooking off the heat, so don't overcook.

ASSEMBLE AND SERVE: While the vegetables are still hot, drizzle with the lemon vinaigrette and finish with freshly grated lemon zest, flaky salt and freshly ground black pepper to taste. Pile high on a serving platter, layering them with fresh herbs and serve additional dressing on the side.

ROASTED WINTER VEG

For the Harissa Seasoning Blend

2 tablespoons chilli powder

1 tablespoon ground cumin

1 tablespoon ground coriander

1 tablespoon caraway seeds

1 tablespoon smoked paprika

2 teaspoons garlic powder

1 teaspoon dried oregano

1 teaspoon kosher salt

For the Veg

1 medium winter squash, such as butternut, kabocha, or acorn, peeled, halved, and deseeded

3 medium carrots, peeled

1 medium parsnip, peeled

1 medium red onion, peeled and quartered

3 tablespoons extra-virgin olive oil

1 tablespoon Harissa Seasoning or store-bought spice blend of your choice

Radicchio or other bitter lettuces, for serving

1 lemon, for serving

Chopped fresh flat-leaf parsley leaves, radicchio, or any bitter lettuces, for serving

Kosher salt and freshly ground black pepper

Serves 4 to 6

Part 3 of the key veg-cooking techniques is roasting. One of my red flags is that I don't really love a roasted vegetable. I prefer my veg to be bright and crunchy and seasoned with a ton of acid (see Blanched Spring Veg, page 108) and roasted vegetables are often the opposite of that. Once in a while, though, the craving strikes for a comforting plate of creamy, soft, caramelized winter vegetables like carrots, parsnips, or squash, and this is the recipe I reach for. Think of it as your back-pocket, one-pan blueprint for which you don't need much more than olive oil, salt, pepper, and 30 minutes. But I like making things a touch more interesting with my slightly spicy harissa seasoning blend and crisp radicchio for freshness.

Preheat the oven to 220°C. Place two roasting trays in the oven while it heats.

MAKE THE SEASONING: Combine all ingredients in a bowl.

PREP THE VEG: Cut your veg into semi-uniform pieces, 1 to 2 inches. Transfer them to a large bowl and add the olive oil, 2 tablespoons harissa seasoning, a generous pinch of salt, and a few cracks of pepper. Toss to coat.

ROAST THE VEG: Carefully remove the roasting trays from the oven and spread the veg in a single layer.

Roast, flipping once three-quarters of the way through, until the veg is fork-tender and beginning to caramelize, 25 to 35 minutes. Taste for salt and adjust as needed.

SERVE: Transfer the veg to a bowl along with the radicchio, grated lemon zest, a squeeze of lemon juice, a pinch of flaky salt, and fresh chopped parsley. Toss to combine. Plate and serve.

BROWN BUTTERED BROCCOLI

½ stick (4 tablespoons) salted butter, cubed

Kosher salt

1 pound Tenderstem broccoli, trimmed

1 lemon, zested and halved

Flaky salt and freshly ground black pepper

Serves 4

Something I often remind myself when developing recipes: making something different doesn't always make it better. Could I have given the buttered broccoli that I grew up with a full head-to-toe makeover? Sure. But sometimes, a dish doesn't need a makeover, it just needs to play dress up. And if we're being honest, a bowl of buttered broccoli (or slightly more posh Tenderstem broccoli, in this case) is often all you need, especially on a busy weeknight or for a dinner party where you're serving five million other things. But we can still pamper her with some fun accessories like flaky salt, lemon zest, and extra-virgin olive oil.

FOR THE BROWN BUTTER: Heat a small saucepan over medium heat. Add the butter and cook, stirring occasionally, until it begins to foam, about 5 minutes. When the foaming and bubbling settle down, continue to cook until the butter smells nutty and the milk solids are nicely browned at the bottom of the pan, about 2 minutes more. Turn off the heat and set aside.

FOR BLANCHED BROCCOLI: In a large pot, bring 5 quarts of water and 1 tablespoon of kosher salt to a boil. While the water comes to a boil, prep an ice bath. In a large bowl, combine a couple handfuls of ice with enough cold water to cover.

Add the veg to the boiling water and cook for 2 minutes or until the stalks are tender. Use tongs to transfer the broccoli to the ice bath until cooled, about 3 minutes. Drain and pat dry.

SERVE: Transfer the broccoli to a plate and pour over the brown butter. Finish with lemon zest, a squeeze of lemon juice, a sprinkle of flaky salt, and a few cracks of pepper.

HOT TIP

Ways to remix this dish include, but are not limited to: add a tablespoon of miso to the brown butter, use chilli-infused olive oil, add chilli crisp, finish with a dusting of Parmesan cheese, swap balsamic vinegar for lemon. Plus, trade in any tender green veg, such as asparagus, sugar snap peas, or broccoli. Flavour opportunities are limited only by your imagination and pantry.

TOMATOES AND CORN

4 ears sweet corn, kernels cut from the cobs

2 pints cherry tomatoes, halved

2 tablespoons chilli-infused olive oil

½ teaspoon flaky salt

1 lemon

1 cup packed fresh basil leaves, torn in 1-inch pieces

2 tablespoons finely chopped fresh chives

Serves 4 to 6

I first made this dish one August afternoon while working as a private chef, when the cherry tomato yield from the garden was so abundant I was borderline desperate to use them up in a timely fashion. And as the saying goes, what grows together goes together, so I recruited fellow star summer veg, sweet corn, to join the party. Since it was peak summer, the tomatoes were too juicy and the corn too sweet to be anything other than their best selves. I've dolled them up a touch with (store-bought) chilli-infused oil and a sprinkle of fresh herbs, but otherwise let their flavours say what they need to say.

ASSEMBLE AND SERVE: In a large bowl, combine the corn, tomatoes, olive oil, flaky salt, and a squeeze of lemon juice. Toss to coat. Gently fold in the herbs. Transfer to a serving bowl.

HOT TIP

If you can't find chilli-infused olive oil at the store, you can sub with extra-virgin olive oil and a pinch of chilli flakes for heat.

ASPARAGUS FRIES WITH FETA

1 pound asparagus, woody ends trimmed

4 ounces fresh sheep's milk feta cheese, preferably in brine (about ¾ cup)

1 teaspoon dried oregano

1 lemon, zested and sliced into wedges

Extra-virgin olive oil

Kosher salt and freshly ground black pepper

Serves 4 to 6

On my first trip to Greece I was introduced to Greek fries, a beautiful combination of crispy French fries smothered in fresh sheep's milk feta and oregano. Since I love eating super-crunchy asparagus spears with my hands, I got the idea to give my lightly roasted (emphasis on lightly—no limp asparagus here) veg its Mediterranean moment. Yes, you can use any other tender green vegetables here; no, you cannot use pre-crumbled feta cheese. Okay, fine, technically you can; but it's not nearly as plump and creamy as feta in brine or a vacuum-packed sheep's milk feta. NOW BEFORE YOU GET MAD, this dish is not meant to be a substitute for French fries, but rather to be eaten like French fries (that is, with your hands). So by all means, make this recipe with fried potatoes instead, if you so please.

ROAST THE ASPARAGUS: Preheat the oven to 220°C. If your oven has a fan setting (popularly known as "air-frying"), use that. Arrange the asparagus in a roasting tray, drizzle with the olive oil, or more as needed to coat, and season with a generous pinch of salt and a few cracks of pepper. Toss until well coated.

Roast until the asparagus is just barely tender. For skinny spears, timing will be 5 to 7 minutes and for thicker spears, it will be closer to 8 to 10 minutes. If in doubt, underdo it—you want asparagus that stands straight up after roasting.

SERVE: Break apart the feta into small crumbles. Transfer the asparagus to a serving dish and top with crumbled feta, oregano, freshly grated lemon zest, and a couple cracks of pepper. Serve with wedges of lemon.

ROASTED BROCCOLI WITH CAPER BUTTER

2 medium heads of broccoli

1 tablespoon extra-virgin olive oil

½ stick (4 tablespoons) unsalted butter, chilled, cut in 4 tablespoon-size pieces

1 medium garlic clove, peeled and finely grated

2 tablespoons capers in brine, drained, plus 1 tablespoon caper brine

1 lemon, juiced (about 2 to 3 tablespoons)

Kosher salt

Serves 4 to 6

Roasting broccoli in large pieces rather than in tiny florets gives you that perfect caramelized crispiness without completely drying out the centre. And dousing roasted broccoli in salty, garlicky caper butter gives you a veg side reminiscent of my fave chicken picatta.

Preheat the oven to 230°C. Place a roasting tray in the oven while it preheats.

PREP THE BROCCOLI: Slice the broccoli into quarters, keeping the florets attached to the stem. Put the broccoli in a large bowl along with the olive oil and a small pinch of salt (the sauce will be salty so go light here). Toss until well coated.

ROAST THE BROCCOLI: Carefully remove the roasting tray from the oven and place the broccoli on the roasting tray, cut side down. Return the roasting tray to the oven and cook until the bottom of the broccoli is caramelized and the stems are fork-tender, 25 to 30 minutes.

MAKE THE SAUCE: In a small saucepan over medium-high heat, melt 1 tablespoon of the butter. Add the garlic and cook for about 30 seconds, then add the capers. Continue cooking for another minute, and then add the brine.

Reduce the heat to low and start whisking in the remaining 3 tablespoons of butter, 1 tablespoon at a time. When all of the butter has been added and the sauce is emulsified, turn off the heat and whisk in 2 tablespoons of lemon juice.

SERVE: Plate the broccoli and drizzle over the sauce.

CHILLI-BRAISED CAULIFLOWER

2 tablespoons extra-virgin olive oil

2 medium garlic cloves, peeled

2 tablespoons chopped Calabrian chillies

2 tablespoons Champagne vinegar

1 teaspoon Dijon mustard

1 teaspoon fish sauce

1 medium head cauliflower, cut into 6 wedges

Kosher salt and freshly ground black pepper

Serves 4 to 6

I'm what you would call a reluctant cauliflower lover; it's just not what usually does it for me. BUT, chunked into wedges and braised low and slow in a garlicky Calabrian chilli-Dijon sort-of vinaigrette so all those flavours seep into the veg? That almost *makes me want to take back everything I had to say about cauliflower. (Except that it should never be a pizza crust. Or a steak.) You can sub in florets, if that's easier for you, or swap in other sturdy veg like carrots or parsnips.*

Preheat the oven to 220°C.

BLEND THE CHILLI GARLIC SAUCE: In a blender, combine 1 tablespoon of olive oil with the garlic, chillies, vinegar, mustard, and fish sauce. Blend until smooth.

COOK THE CAULIFLOWER: In a large cast-iron casserole dish or braiser, heat 1 tablespoon olive oil over medium-high heat. When the oil shimmers, working in batches, sear the cauliflower cut side down until golden brown, about 3 minutes.

Pour in the chilli-garlic sauce, cover tightly with a lid, and transfer to the oven to braise until tender, 15 to 20 minutes. If the sauce starts to stick to the bottom of the pan, stir in a splash of water.

SERVE: Transfer the cauliflower to a serving plate and spoon over the sauce.

DUCK FAT POTATOES

3 pounds russet potatoes, peeled and cut into 3-inch pieces

¼ cup duck fat

4 sprigs fresh rosemary

Kosher and flaky salt

Serves 4 to 6

The British certainly get one thing right and that's a crispy roast potato. Their secret? Duck fat (or goose fat). What you get are a fluffy mashed potato-like interior and super crispy, crunchy outside. It's officially the only way to properly cook potatoes (unless you're mashing them, in which case proceed to page 127).

Preheat the oven to 220°C. Place a large cast-iron pan or cast-iron baking dish in the oven as it preheats.

PAR-COOK THE POTATOES: Put the potatoes in a large pot and add cold water to cover by at least 1 inch. Add kosher salt and bring the water to a boil. Reduce to a simmer and cook until the potatoes are tender on the outside but not fully cooked in the centre, about 8 minutes. Drain the potatoes in a colander and let them sit for 2 minutes, giving them a shake every now and then. This releases more of the steam, and also roughs up the exterior of the potatoes, adding little nooks and crannies to the surface that will turn into crispy bits as they roast.

ROAST THE POTATOES: Remove the pan from the oven, add the duck fat, and then transfer back to the oven until the duck fat has melted. Remove the roasting pan and add the potatoes and a generous pinch of kosher salt. Toss the potatoes to coat them with duck fat, then spread them in a single layer.

Roast until the potatoes are golden brown and crispy, about 40 minutes, flipping them and adding the rosemary halfway through.

SERVE: Transfer the hot potatoes to a serving platter and finish with a good punch of flaky salt.

HOT TIP

Some grocery stores now carry duck fat, but if yours doesn't check your local butcher or specialty food shop. Online ordering is always an option, too. You can also reuse the duck fat from my duck confit recipe (page 207). Bacon drippings work, too, although they will give a stronger, smokier flavour. And yes, fine, you could use vegetable oil.

A GOOD MASH

1½ pounds baby yellow potatoes, scrubbed

¾ cup double cream

2 tablespoons unsalted butter

¼ cup crème fraîche

¼ cup chopped fresh chives

Kosher salt and freshly ground black pepper

Serves 4 to 6

I've been exclusively preparing the same mashed potato recipe since culinary school. It involves peeling potatoes, boiling them, passing them through a potato ricer, and steeping the milk and butter. While, yes, this gives you a perfectly smooth and creamy potato puree, it also takes hours to prepare and creates more dishes than I care to wash in one night. So I dumped the perfect potatoes for this lovable lumpy mash that puts me, and my time, first.

COOK THE POTATOES: Place the potatoes in a medium or large saucepan, cover with 1 inch of cold water, and add 1 tablespoon of salt. Bring to a boil, then lower the heat to a simmer. Simmer until the potatoes are fork-tender, 10 to 15 minutes.

While the potatoes simmer, combine the cream and butter in a small saucepan. Cook over low heat until the butter melts. Keep warm over very low heat until you're ready to add to the potatoes, stirring occasionally so that the bottom doesn't scorch.

MASH THE POTATOES: Drain the potatoes and return them to the pot. Add the cream and butter mixture plus 1 teaspoon of salt and a couple cracks of pepper. Use a potato masher to mash the potatoes until creamy, but don't overmix. Use a rubber spatula to fold in the crème fraîche until well combined, then fold in the chives. Taste and season with more salt and/or pepper, if needed.

noodles

BUCATINI AND MEATBALLS

For the Meatballs

1 batch Classic Red Sauce (recipe follows) or 6 cups pre-made sauce

1 tablespoon extra-virgin olive oil, plus more as needed

½ medium yellow onion, peeled and finely chopped (about ⅓ cup)

½ cup dry red wine, such as Chianti, or water

½ cup panko bread crumbs

⅓ cup whole-milk ricotta cheese, plus more for serving

1 ounce freshly grated Parmesan cheese (about ¼ cup)

¼ cup fresh flat-leaf parsley, finely chopped

1 medium egg, lightly beaten

2 medium garlic cloves, peeled and finely chopped

1 teaspoon chopped Calabrian chillies

1 teaspoon dried oregano

1 pound lean beef mince

Kosher salt and freshly ground black pepper

For the Pasta

2 tablespoons kosher salt

1 pound bucatini pasta

1 tablespoon unsalted butter

2 tablespoons freshly grated Parmesan cheese, plus more for serving

1 cup packed fresh basil leaves, plus more for serving

Serves 6 (makes 20 meatballs)

Spaghetti and meatballs has been my favourite food ever since I can remember, and while I can appreciate a plate of meatballs the size of tennis balls, these are not them. These are weeknight-friendly meatballs crafted to be perfectly petite, simmered in sauce instead of fried, and nestled atop a plate of saucy pasta. And in case you missed the other thoughtful touches here, the recipe has been strategically portioned to involve one batch of sauce, one pound of pasta, and one pound of meat—the perfect ratio to make enough for leftovers, but not so much that you're left to deal with a week's worth.

Start preparing the Classic Red Sauce or transfer your pre-made sauce to a large pot or cast-iron casserole dish. Preheat the grill on high.

SAUTÉ THE ONIONS FOR THE MEATBALLS: Heat a large cast-iron casserole dish over medium heat and add the olive oil. When it shimmers, add the onion and cook, stirring occasionally, until softened, 5 to 7 minutes. Pour in the wine and cook until the liquid has almost completely evaporated, about 4 minutes. Turn off the heat and transfer the onions to a large bowl to cool slightly.

MAKE THE MEATBALLS: When the onions have cooled, add the panko, ricotta, Parm, parsley, egg, garlic, Calabrian chillies, oregano, 1 teaspoon kosher salt, and a couple cracks of pepper and thoroughly mix until fully combined. Add the beef mince and gently mix together with your hands until homogeneous. Don't overwork at this point or you'll end up with tough meatballs.

GRILL THE MEATBALLS: Brush a roasting tray with olive oil.

Use a 2-ounce cookie scoop or ¼ cup measuring cup to portion out the meatballs. Coat your hands in olive oil and roll meatballs that are about the size of golf balls. Arrange them on the prepared roasting tray and grill until browned, 5 to 7 minutes. Lower the oven to 90°C.

SIMMER THE MEATBALLS: Bring the sauce to a simmer over medium-high heat, then adjust the heat to low. Carefully nestle the meatballs into the sauce in a single layer, cover, and simmer until they're cooked through, 15 to 20 minutes. (Resist the urge to stir; the meatballs will be very delicate.) Using a slotted spoon, transfer the cooked meatballs to a platter, cover tightly with foil, and transfer to the oven to keep warm.

CONTINUED

BUCATINI AND MEATBALLS

CONTINUED

COOK THE PASTA: In a large pot, bring five quarts of water to a boil and add 2 tablespoons of salt. Add the pasta and cook for 1 to 2 minutes shy of the package instructions.

Use tongs to transfer the cooked pasta directly into the sauce, along with ¼ cup of pasta water. Bring to a simmer and finish cooking the pasta in the sauce until al dente, 1 to 2 minutes. Turn off the heat and stir in the butter, Parm, and additional pasta water if needed to help loosen the sauce. Fold in the basil right before serving.

SERVE: Plate the pasta, top with meatballs, a sprinkle of Parm, a dollop of ricotta, and more basil.

CLASSIC RED SAUCE

¼ cup extra-virgin olive oil

½ medium yellow onion, peeled and finely chopped

5 garlic cloves, peeled and finely chopped

2 (28-ounce) cans whole peeled tomatoes

Handful of fresh basil leaves

Pinch of dried Italian oregano

1½ teaspoons kosher salt, plus more to taste

Makes about 6 cups

Heat a large cast-iron casserole dish over medium-low heat. Combine the olive oil and onion and cook until soft but not brown. Add the garlic and cook, stirring, until fragrant, 1 minute more.

Reduce the heat to low and add the tomatoes. Using a wooden spoon, crush the tomatoes into smaller chunks. Increase the heat to high and bring to a boil; then adjust the heat to low and let simmer, uncovered, stirring occasionally, until the sauce has thickened and deepened in flavour, 40 to 45 minutes. Use an immersion blender to blend the sauce to your desired consistency.

Stir in the basil, oregano, and salt and allow the sauce to simmer just long enough for the flavours to meld, about 1 more minute. Season with more salt, if needed.

Enjoy now or allow the sauce to cool before storing it in a sealed container in the refrigerator for up to 1 week or in the freezer for up to 6 months.

SPICY SQUASH PASTA

2 to 3 medium honeynut squash (see Hot Tip), halved lengthwise, seeds removed

6 medium garlic cloves, unpeeled

1 medium shallot, unpeeled and halved

2 tablespoons extra-virgin olive oil

1 teaspoon chicken or vegetable bouillon

¼ teaspoon cayenne pepper, plus more to taste

¼ teaspoon crushed red pepper flakes, plus more to taste

1 pound mezzi rigatoni

2 tablespoons unsalted butter

2 tablespoons Sesame Chilli Crunch (recipe follows) or store-bought

Kosher salt and freshly ground black pepper

Serves 4 to 6

A few years ago I was catering a fancy dinner party tasting menu and prepared a velvety squash puree to accompany an herb roast chicken. When I tasted it, my first thought was, I should put this on some pasta. Because while I can appreciate the art of a good tasting menu, a humble bowl of saucy noodles is much more my speed. This pasta features one of my favourite recipes in the entire book, my Sesame Chilli Crunch. It's nutty, salty, and spicy, and pairs perfectly with the slight sweetness of the roasted squash.

Preheat oven to 190°C.

ROAST THE SQUASH: Arrange the squash, garlic, and shallot on a roasting tray. Coat everything with olive oil and season with salt and pepper. Turn the squash cut side down and roast until it's tender, about 30 minutes. Set aside to cool.

MAKE THE SAUCE: When cool enough to handle, peel the garlic, shallot, and squash and transfer to a blender along with the bouillon, cayenne pepper, pepper flakes, and a pinch of salt and blend until smooth, adding a few tablespoons of water.

COOK THE PASTA: In a large pot, bring five quarts of water to a boil and add 2 tablespoons of salt. Cook the pasta 2 minutes shy of package instructions. Drain the pasta, reserving at least 1 cup of the cooking water.

ASSEMBLE: Add the cooked pasta back to the pot, along with with the squash puree and about ¼ cup of the pasta water. Bring to a simmer and cook the pasta in the sauce for 2 minutes, stirring occasionally. Turn off the heat and fold in the butter, a dash of the sesame chilli crunch, and additional pasta water as needed. Taste and season with salt as needed.

SERVE: Plate the pasta and top with a healthy drizzle of sesame chilli crunch.

HOT TIP
Honeynut squash is similar to butternut squash but is much smaller, sweeter, and more flavourful. If you can't find honeynut squash, you can substitute 1 medium to large butternut squash and increase the roasting time as needed, removing the garlic and shallots partially through the cook time so that they don't burn.

CONTINUED

SPICY SQUASH PASTA

CONTINUED

SESAME CHILLI CRUNCH

¼ cup crushed red pepper flakes

2 tablespoons white sesame seeds

2 tablespoons black sesame seeds

1 teaspoon sweet paprika

10 medium garlic cloves, peeled

1 medium shallot, halved and peeled

1⅓ cups vegetable oil

1 tablespoon toasted sesame oil

1 tablespoon kosher salt

¼ teaspoon sugar

¼ teaspoon MSG

3 tablespoons soy sauce

2 teaspoons rice vinegar

Makes 2 cups

HOT TIP
Any dried crushed red pepper will work here, like Sichuan chilli flakes, chilli de arbol, gochugaru, and more.

HOT TIP
For those unfamiliar with salsa macha, it's quite similar to a Chinese chilli crisp in that it's a crunchy chilli and oil based condiment, but uses Mexican chillies and has the addition of nuts (like peanuts) and seeds (like sesame seeds).

Now I like spicy things, but condiments like chilli crisp and salsa macha (see Hot Tip) can be too spicy for me. So I sought to make a condiment that was umami- and crunch-forward, with just a mild hint of spice. Thus, the Sesame Chilli Crunch was born! With that said, if you're looking for mouth-numbing heat, this recipe will not provide that for you. But feel free to go off script and up the pepper count if you so desire.

PREP: In a medium heatproof bowl, combine the red pepper flakes, white and black sesame seeds, and paprika. Fit a fine-mesh sieve over the bowl and set aside.

Using a food processor, chop the garlic and shallot by pulsing the machine on and off.

FRY THE AROMATICS: In a small saucepan, combine the vegetable oil, garlic, and shallot. Heat over medium-low heat until the oil starts to bubble. Let the mixture sizzle, occasionally stirring and scraping any bits from the sides or the bottom of the pot, until the garlic just begins to brown, 10 to 15 minutes.

STRAIN: Immediately strain the hot oil mixture through the sieve over the pepper flakes. Transfer the fried garlic and shallots to a kitchen towel-lined plate to cool. (The hot oil activates the heat and flavours of the chilli flakes; straining out the garlic and shallots will keep them crispy.) Let cool for 30 minutes.

ASSEMBLE: When the oil has cooled, add the garlic and shallots back to the oil mixture along with sesame oil, salt, sugar, and MSG. Wait to add the soy sauce and vinegar until right before you're ready to use, as this will shorten the shelf life of the chilli crunch and make the crispy garlic and shallots go soggy.

Measure approximately how much chilli crunch you'll need for one sitting into a separate container, then add soy sauce and vinegar. For example, if you're using 2 tablespoons of sesame chilli crunch, mix in about ½ teaspoon soy sauce, and ⅛ teaspoon rice vinegar.

This may seem over the top, but it's worth it to preserve the integrity and longevity of the crunch. Plus the soy adds a great salty depth of flavour while the vinegar brings a much needed hit of acid.

FOR STORAGE: *With* soy sauce and vinegar, this will keep in an airtight container in the fridge for 3 days. *Without* soy sauce and rice vinegar, this will keep in an airtight container in the fridge for 2 weeks or longer.

ZITI ALLA ZOZZONA

4 ounces guanciale, cut into fine matchsticks

8 ounces hot Italian sausage, casing removed

1 small yellow onion, peeled and finely chopped

2 medium garlic cloves, peeled and finely chopped

¼ cup tomato paste

2 (14-ounce) can whole peeled tomatoes, crushed

1 tablespoon chopped Calabrian chillies

1 Parmesan cheese rind (optional)

1 pound tubular pasta, such as ziti rigati

4 medium egg yolks

1 ounce freshly grated pecorino Romano or Parmesan cheese, (about ¼ cup), plus more for serving

Extra-virgin olive oil

Kosher salt and freshly ground pepper

Serves 4 to 6

Pasta alla zozzona is the perfect marriage of four traditional Roman pastas: cacio e pepe (pecorino and black pepper), carbonara (egg yolk-thickened sauce with pecorino, black pepper, and guanciale), Amatriciana (spicy tomatoes, guanciale, pecorino, and black pepper), and Gricia (guanciale, pecorino, and black pepper)—plus spicy sausage. It's a "kitchen sink" dish that's the antithesis of simplicity-always Italian cooking, but if there's anything that will always go well with pasta, it's maximalism. And who am I to argue with the Romans?

FIRST MAKE THE RED SAUCE: Add the guanciale and a splash of olive oil to a cold cast-iron casserole dish. Heat over medium-low and cook until the fat has rendered and the guanciale is crispy, about 7 minutes. Turn off the heat, remove the guanciale from the pan with a slotted spoon, and set it aside. Pour the rendered fat into a separate container, leaving behind enough to coat the bottom of the pot.

Increase the heat to medium-high and add the sausage in 2- to 3-inch pieces. Sear until the sausage is golden brown and caramelized, about 5 minutes. Break up the sausage into a fine mince. Once cooked through, remove from the pot with a slotted spoon and add it to the guanciale. Set aside.

Return the pot to medium-high heat and add the onion along with 1 tablespoon of the reserved drippings and a pinch of salt. (But not too much because the pork and the Parm are salty.) Cook, stirring occasionally and using your spoon to scrape up any brown bits from the bottom of the pan, until the onions are soft and translucent, about 3 minutes. Add the garlic and cook, stirring, until fragrant, about 1 minute.

Stir in the tomato paste and cook, stirring, until caramelized and sticking to the bottom of the pan, about 3 minutes. Stir in the tomatoes and Calabrian chillies plus the sausage and guanciale. Add the Parmesan rind (if using) and bring to a gentle simmer. Reduce heat to low, partially cover with a lid, and cook, stirring occasionally, for 30 to 45 minutes. Turn off the heat and remove and discard the Parm rind.

CONTINUED

ZITI ALLA ZOZZONA

CONTINUED

COOK THE PASTA: In a large pot, bring five quarts of water to a boil and add 2 tablespoons of salt. Cook the pasta for 2 minutes shy of the package instructions.

MAKE THE CHEESE MIXTURE: In a large heatproof bowl, whisk together the egg yolks, cheese, and lots of black pepper. Gradually whisk in ¼ cup of the hot pasta water until fully combined. Make sure to use hot water and keep the whisking going. This tempers the eggs and keeps them from scrambling in the sauce.

SAUCE THE PASTA: Use a slotted spoon to transfer the pasta directly into the tomato sauce. Simmer the pasta in the sauce until al dente, about 2 minutes.

Turn off the heat and immediately stir in the cheese-and-egg mixture. Continue to mix until emulsified.

SERVE: Transfer the pasta to bowls and top with more grated cheese and ground pepper.

SHORT RIB BOLOGNESE

2 pounds boneless beef short ribs, beef chuck, or beef stew meat, cut into 2-inch cubes or 3½ pounds of bone-in beef short ribs

2 tablespoons plain flour

1 tablespoon vegetable oil

8 ounces pancetta, diced small

1 medium yellow onion, peeled and roughly chopped

3 small carrots, peeled and roughly chopped

2 celery stalks, roughly chopped

¼ cup tomato paste

2 cups dry white wine, such as Pinot Grigio

4 cups chicken stock

1 dried or fresh bay leaf

½ cup double cream

Pinch of freshly grated nutmeg

2 pounds short pasta, such as casarecce (see Hot Tip)

½ stick (4 tablespoons) unsalted butter

1 ounce freshly grated Parmesan cheese (about ¼ cup)

Kosher salt and freshly ground black pepper

Serves 8 to 10

A traditional beef bolognese is up there in my top three favourite pastas of all time (next to spaghetti and meatballs, and lobster capellini). It's the perfect marriage of white wine braised meat in a slightly creamy slightly tomato-y gravy. And as hard as it is to improve on perfection, I at least had to try. Here, I've traded (one might say upgraded) beef mince for falling-apart tender beef short ribs that release deep, rich flavour as they simmer. This recipe makes enough sauce to coat 2 pounds of pasta. That's about 10 servings. While you can technically halve the sauce recipe, if you want to make less pasta, I recommend making a full batch of sauce and freezing half to save for a rainy day. You'll thank me, and yourself, later.

Preheat the oven to 150°C.

BROWN THE MEAT: Arrange the beef in a roasting tray, pat dry with a paper towel, lightly dust with flour, and season with about 2 teaspoons kosher salt.

Heat a large cast-iron casserole dish over medium-high heat, then add the vegetable oil. Working in batches, sear the beef until caramelized on all sides, about 3 minutes per side. Return the browned beef to the roasting tray and set aside.

Drain any excess fat from the pot, leaving just enough to coat the bottom. Reduce the heat to medium-low and add the pancetta to the pot. Cook, stirring occasionally, until it is crisp and golden brown, about 8 minutes.

CHOP AND SAUTÉ THE VEG: While the meat is browning, add the onions, carrots, and celery to a food processor and process until finely chopped, scraping down the sides of the bowl with a spatula as needed.

Increase the heat to medium-high and add the chopped vegetables to the pot with the pancetta along with a pinch of salt and cook until they have softened and released most of their moisture, about 5 minutes. Stir in the tomato paste. Cook, stirring occasionally, until the vegetables are soft and the tomato paste begins to brown, about 5 minutes.

BRAISE THE BEEF: Pour in the wine and use a wooden spoon to scrape up the brown bits from the bottom of the pot. Add the beef back to the pot, bring the mixture to a simmer, and cook, uncovered, until the wine has almost completely evaporated, about 15 minutes.

CONTINUED

SHORT RIB BOLOGNESE

CONTINUED

Add the stock and the bay leaf, gently stir to combine, and bring the mixture to a low boil. Turn off the heat. Cover tightly with a lid and transfer the pot to the oven. Bake until the beef is fork-tender, about 2½ to 3 hours for boneless beef and 3 hours for bone-in short ribs.

FINISH THE SAUCE: Once the beef is done braising, remove the bay leaf and discard. Use tongs to remove the pieces of beef from the pot and transfer into a large mixing bowl or onto a cutting board. Use forks to shred the beef, then return it to the sauce. Stir in the double cream and nutmeg. Taste and adjust with salt and pepper as needed. Heat over a low simmer while you cook the pasta.

COOK THE PASTA: In a large pot, bring five quarts of water to a boil and add 2 tablespoons of salt. Add the pasta and cook for 2 minutes shy of the package instructions.

SAUCE THE PASTA: Use a kitchen spider or slotted spoon to transfer the pasta directly to the simmering sauce along with ¼ cup of pasta water. Let the pasta and sauce simmer together for 2 minutes, stirring occasionally.

Turn off the heat and stir in the butter, Parm, and additional pasta water if needed to help loosen the sauce.

SERVE: Plate the pasta and top with Parmesan and freshly ground black pepper.

HOT TIP
If you're serving fewer people, make only 1 pound of pasta and transfer half of the sauce into airtight containers and store in the fridge for up to 3 days or the freezer for 6 months.

BROCCOLI CAVATELLI

4 cups broccoli florets

4 cups packed fresh spinach leaves

1 pound cavatelli pasta

1 cup Basil Parsley Pesto (recipe follows) or store-bought

1 teaspoon chicken bouillon base (I use Better than Bouillon), plus more to taste

1 lemon, zested

3 tablespoons unsalted butter (optional)

Freshly grated Parmesan cheese, for serving

Kosher salt and freshly ground black pepper

Serves 4 to 6

HOT TIP

You'll notice that although all of my other pasta recipes include butter, it's listed as optional here. The dish is great without it, thanks to the pop of umami from chicken bouillon. But I just can't help myself now can I? After all, everything's better with butter.

Believe it or not, I was a very picky eater as a child, but the two foods that I LOVED were buttered noodles and broccoli. Unsurprisingly, my mom's broccoli cavatelli was one of my all-time favourites, so it only made sense to include it here too. The basic ingredients remain the same (aromatics, broccoli, chicken stock, Parm, and cavatelli), and it still has all the simplicity of a weeknight meal that can be prepared just after walking in the door from work, but elevated just a touch with a pureed broccoli pesto sauce. I also like to puree the broccoli into a creamy sauce (notice a theme here??), which means you get all that flavour in every bite. This also doubles as a fantastic way to sneak more veggies into the meals of picky eaters, from toddlers to grown-ups.

BLANCH THE VEG AND BOIL THE PASTA: In a large pot, bring five quarts of water to a boil and add 2 tablespoons of salt. Add the broccoli to the boiling water and cook until the broccoli is bright green and tender but still firm, about 2 minutes. Add the spinach and cook just until it begins to wilt, about 30 seconds more. Use a kitchen spider or slotted spoon to transfer the broccoli and spinach from the boiling water to a bowl. Set aside to cool.

Add the pasta to the same pot of boiling water and cook for about 2 minutes shy of the package instructions.

MAKE THE SAUCE: In a blender or food processor, combine the cooled broccoli and spinach, basil parsley pesto, chicken bouillon, a pinch of salt, and a couple cracks of pepper. Add 2 tablespoons of cooking water and blend until smooth.

ASSEMBLE AND SERVE: When the pasta is done cooking, reserve 1 cup of pasta water, drain, and return the pasta to the pot. Add the broccoli sauce, plus ¼ cup of pasta water. Bring to a simmer and cook the pasta in the sauce for 2 minutes, stirring occasionally and adding more pasta water as needed.

Turn off the heat and fold in the lemon zest and butter (if using). Plate the pasta and top with Parm and black pepper.

CONTINUED

BROCCOLI CAVATELLI

CONTINUED

BASIL PARSLEY PESTO

6 cups packed fresh basil leaves (about 3½ ounces or 100 grams)

2 cups packed fresh parsley leaves (about 1¾ ounces or 50 grams)

½ cup pine nuts

2 medium garlic cloves, peeled

1 cup extra-virgin olive oil, plus more as needed

½ cup freshly grated Parmesan cheese (about 2 ounces or 60 grams)

½ cup freshly grated pecorino Romano cheese (about 2 ounces or 60 grams)

Zest of 1 lemon (optional)

Kosher salt

Makes about 3 cups

BLANCH THE HERBS: Add ice to a large bowl and fill with cold water. Set aside.

Bring a large pot of water to a boil. Add the basil and parsley and blanch until they turn bright green, about 30 seconds. Use a sieve to transfer them to the ice bath. Let them cool down for 30 seconds then drain well. Squeeze out the excess moisture. Set aside.

TOAST THE PINE NUTS: In a small frying pan, toast the pine nuts over medium heat, watching closely and shaking the pan to prevent burning, until golden brown, 5 to 7 minutes. Let cool slightly.

MAKE THE PESTO: In a food processor, combine the toasted pine nuts and garlic and process until a paste forms. Add the blanched herbs and pulse while slowly streaming in the olive oil.

Process until the mixture is smooth and homogenous, scraping down the sides of the bowl with a spatula as needed. Add both cheeses, the lemon zest (if using), and a pinch of salt and pulse just to combine. Taste and season with more salt, if needed.

Transfer the pesto to sealed containers and drizzle a layer of olive oil over the top, which will keep it from browning. Store in the fridge for up to 2 weeks or in the freezer for up to 6 months.

HOT TIP

I've included weight measurements for the herbs in this recipe because I feel like cup measures for herbs can be too variable. Normally, it doesn't bother me, but with pesto it's important to keep the ingredient ratios consistent. If you don't have a scale, don't worry about it. It truly is not that big of a deal (nothing ever is).

HOT TIP

Blanching the herbs ensures that the pesto stays a vivid green colour, but this technically is optional.

BAKED CRAB MAC AND CHEESE

2 tablespoons unsalted butter

2 medium garlic cloves, peeled and finely grated

2 tablespoons plain flour

½ cup dry white wine, such as Pinot Grigio

1 cup whole milk

1 cup double cream

5 ounces freshly grated Gruyère cheese (about 1¼ cups)

5 ounces freshly grated sharp white Cheddar cheese (about 1¼ cups)

2 ounces freshly grated Parmesan cheese (about ½ cup)

½ cup finely chopped fresh chives, plus more for serving

1 teaspoon Dijon mustard

1 lemon, zested

8 ounces medium shell pasta

8 ounces white crabmeat

1 cup Toasted Garlic Panko (page 31)

Kosher salt and freshly ground black pepper

Serves 4 to 6

This is the grown-up mac & cheese of my dreams. The cheese sauce starts with white wine, which is always a good sign. We then melt together a blend of Cheddar for the quintessential mac flavour, Gruyère for its ideal melting consistency, and Parm for some salty complexity. Decadent, sweet white crabmeat is folded into the mac, then it's topped with an addictively crunchy layer of Toasted Garlic Panko. This is the kind of dish that makes you want to file your taxes on time—or at the very least bring the perfect side to your next barbecue.

Preheat the oven to 190°C.

MAKE THE CHEESE SAUCE: Heat a large cast-iron casserole dish over medium-high heat and add the butter. When the butter has melted, add the garlic and cook until fragrant, about 1 minute. Add the flour and whisk to incorporate. Continue whisking as you cook off the raw flavour of the flour, about 1 minute. Keep up the whisking as you pour in the wine and cook until the liquid has almost completely evaporated, about 3 minutes.

Gradually whisk in the milk and cream and allow the mixture to come to a simmer. Gradually whisk in the Gruyère, Cheddar, and Parm and continue whisking until the cheese has melted and no lumps remain. Whisk in the chives, mustard, lemon zest, ¼ teaspoon of salt, and a couple cracks of pepper. Taste and season with more salt and/or pepper, if needed. Turn off the heat and set aside.

COOK THE PASTA: In a large pot, bring five quarts of water to a boil and add 2 tablespoons of salt. Add the pasta and cook for 2 minutes shy of the package instructions.

ASSEMBLE THE MAC: Use a slotted spoon to transfer the pasta directly to the sauce and toss to coat. Gently fold in the crabmeat, being careful not to break up any big chunks. The sauce will look loose but it tightens up as it bakes.

Transfer the mac to a 3-quart baking dish. Clean up the edges, and top with the toasted garlic panko.

Bake until golden brown and bubbling, 20 to 25 minutes. Allow the mac to cool for 10 minutes before serving.

SERVE: Sprinkle with more chives and serve.

LOBSTER CAPELLINI

½ stick (4 tablespoons) unsalted butter

2 tablespoons extra-virgin olive oil

4 medium garlic cloves, peeled and thinly sliced

¼ teaspoon crushed red pepper flakes

2 cups cherry tomatoes, halved

¾ pound capellini, or angel hair pasta or spaghetti

8 ounces cooked lobster meat, or meat from 1 (1½-pound) lobster (see page 62)

1 cup loosely packed fresh basil leaves, plus more for serving

¼ cup fresh tarragon, plus more for serving

½ lemon, zested

Kosher salt

Serves 4 to 6

This is a twenty-minute pasta dish that tastes like a million bucks. The secret is pre-cooked lobster meat (which yes, might run you a million bucks but shrimp also does the trick) and the quick cooking of capellini. I used to be a hater of capellini and angel hair pasta until I had it with seafood. Something about the thin, delicate (dare I say limp?) pasta paired with a simple pomodoro butter sauce and tender lobster meat just makes sense to me.

MAKE THE SAUCE: Heat a large cast-iron casserole dish over medium heat and add the butter and olive oil. When the butter has melted, add the garlic and red pepper flakes and cook, stirring, until just softened, 1 to 2 minutes.

Add the tomatoes and a pinch of salt and simmer, stirring occasionally, for 10 to 15 minutes.

Use the back of your spoon to smash some of the tomatoes to release their juices as they cook, but leave some tomatoes intact.

WHILE THE SAUCE SIMMERS, COOK THE PASTA: In a large pot, bring five quarts of water to a boil and add 2 tablespoons of salt. Cook the pasta for 1 minute shy of the package instructions for al dente.

ASSEMBLE: Use tongs to transfer the drained pasta directly to the simmering sauce along with a splash of the cooking water. Let the pasta simmer in the sauce for about a minute, stirring occasionally.

If using pre-cooked lobster meat that is cold from the fridge, follow the reheating instructions on page 62. If using freshly cooked lobster meat that is still warm, you can skip this step. Add the lobster meat, basil, tarragon, and lemon zest to the pasta and gently toss to combine.

SERVE: Plate the pasta and top with fresh herbs.

PINK LEMON PASTA

1 tablespoon whole pink or black peppercorns, plus more for serving

1 pound spaghetti

8 tablespoons (1 stick) cold unsalted butter, cubed

4 ounces freshly grated Parmesan cheese (about 1 cup), plus more for serving

2 lemons (pink, if you can find them), zested and juiced (about ¼ cup), plus 1 lemon thinly sliced for garnish

Kosher salt

Serves 4 to 6

If ever there were a recipe to prove how amazingly sophisticated simple can be, as well as demonstrate the sheer magic of a little pasta cooking water, this is it. The combination of that starchy liquid gold plus butter makes a satisfyingly silky sauce that's balanced by a salty punch of Parm, a bright pop of lemon, and floral pink peppercorn heat.

CRUSH THE PEPPERCORNS: With a mortar and pestle, coarsely crush the whole peppercorns. Or, place the peppercorns in a zip-top bag and use the bottom of a frying pan to gently crush.

COOK THE PASTA: In a large pot, bring five quarts of water to a boil over medium-high heat and add 2 tablespoons of salt. Cook the pasta for about 2 minutes shy of the package instructions.

TOAST THE PEPPERCORNS: Heat a large saucepan or pot over medium heat and add 2 tablespoons of butter. Once the butter is melted, stir in the peppercorns and turn off the heat. Set aside until the pasta is done cooking.

SAUCE THE PASTA: Use tongs to transfer the cooked pasta directly to the pan, along with 1 cup of the pasta cooking water and return the pot to medium heat. Simmer for about 2 minutes, stirring occasionally, until the liquid has reduced and thickened slightly. Fold in the remaining cubed butter, a few pieces at a time, until emulsified.

Turn off the heat and add the Parm, lemon juice, most of the lemon zest, and ¼ cup more pasta water. Toss to combine until the cheese has melted and no lumps remain, adding more pasta water as needed.

SERVE: Plate the pasta and top with lots of Parm, more lemon zest, and cracked peppercorns. Garnish with thinly sliced lemons.

SUNGOLD TOMATO PASTA

1 tablespoon extra-virgin olive oil

2 small shallots, peeled and thinly sliced

5 medium garlic cloves, peeled and thinly sliced

4 cups Sungold tomatoes, halved

¼ teaspoon crushed red pepper flakes

1 pound thick-cut spaghetti, preferably bronze-cut

½ stick (4 tablespoons) unsalted butter

1 ounce freshly grated Parmesan cheese (about ¼ cup)

1 cup packed fresh basil leaves, plus more for garnish

Serves 4 to 6

A saucy celebration of peak summer Sungold tomatoes, this minimum-effort pomodoro-esque sauce gets all-day flavour from caramelized shallots and garlic, Parm, and butter. Also, the blender bully (me) is back and begging you to give this sauce a blitz to ensure each noodle is perfectly coated in that glorious golden sauce.

MAKE THE SAUCE: Heat a large cast-iron casserole dish over low heat. Add the olive oil and shallots and cook, stirring, until they begin to caramelize, 5 to 7 minutes. Add the garlic and cook until just barely golden brown, about 1 minute more.

Add the tomatoes and red pepper flakes. Increase the heat to medium-high and cook, smushing the tomatoes with the back of a spoon to release their juices, until the sauce is slightly thickened and jammy, about 10 minutes.

Turn off the heat. Let the sauce cool before using an immersion blender or blender and processing until smooth.

COOK THE PASTA: Fill a large pot with five quarts of water. Bring it to a boil and add 2 tablespoons of salt. Cook the pasta for 2 minutes shy of the package instructions.

SAUCE THE PASTA: Bring the sauce to a simmer over medium-low heat before adding the pasta. Using tongs, transfer the pasta directly to the sauce and add ¼ cup of the cooking water. Cook the pasta in the sauce for 2 minutes, stirring occasionally.

Turn off the heat and add the butter, Parm, and another ¼ cup of cooking water. Stir until the sauce is glossy and emulsified, adding more cooking water as needed. Fold in the fresh basil.

SERVE: Plate the pasta, top with more basil, and serve.

HOT TIP
The term "bronze-cut pasta" refers to pasta that is made using a specific type of machine equipped with an extruder made of bronze. This produces a noodle that has a rough and somewhat porous exterior that is ideal for sauce to cling to. I recommend seeking out this type of pasta for any pasta dish, but in this case specifically because that detail goes a long way in a dish as simple as this one.

WOK LOBSTER

For the Sauce

2 tablespoons soy sauce

1 tablespoon dark soy sauce (or additional regular soy sauce)

2 tablespoons ponzu

2 tablespoons oyster sauce

½ teaspoon toasted sesame oil

For the Stir-Fry

2 (1½-pound) lobsters, cooked (see page 62), or 4 to 6 cooked lobster tails

1 pound fresh lo mein egg noodles or any long noodle

½ stick (4 tablespoons) unsalted butter

2 cups diagonally sliced spring onions (white and green parts separated, about 2 small bunches)

4 medium garlic cloves, peeled and finely grated

2 limes, sliced into wedges, for serving

Serves 4 to 6

HOT TIP

The dark soy sauce gives the noodles great colour and depth of flavour, so I recommend trying to source it. Otherwise, regular soy sauce will work in a pinch.

Normally when my family is on Nantucket, "fine dining" means standing over a communal bowl of steamed clams or mussels while we're still in our bathing suits. But the one dish that would convince my parents, and eventually my brother and me, to leave the beach early for the day, put on actual clothes, and go out to eat was the Wok-Fried Lobster at The Pearl. The original Cantonese-inspired dish consists of salt and pepper-fried lobster piled atop a mountain of lo mein noodles. I've adapted it to be a bit more home-kitchen friendly by calling for steamed lobster instead of fried, but it's just as delicious.

MAKE THE SAUCE: In a medium bowl, whisk together the soy sauce, dark soy sauce, ponzu, oyster sauce, and sesame oil. Set aside.

PREP THE LOBSTER: Follow the lobster tutorial on page 62 for cooking the lobsters. When the lobsters are cool enough to handle, separate the claws and tails from the bodies. Halve the tails lengthwise and crack open the claws and knuckles, leaving the meat in the shell.

COOK THE NOODLES: Cook the noodles according to the package instructions. Drain and rinse with cold water. Set aside.

STIR-FRY: Heat a large wok, large frying pan, or cast-iron casserole dish over medium heat and add the butter. When the butter has melted, add a handful of the spring onion whites and the lobster. Sauté until fragrant and warmed through, about 3 minutes. Transfer the lobster to a bowl and cover tightly with kitchen foil to keep warm.

Keeping the heat on medium, add the remaining spring onion whites and the garlic. Sauté just until fragrant, about 1 minute. Add the noodles and ½ cup of the sauce, toss to coat and turn off the heat. Fold in half of the spring onion greens.

SERVE: Plate the noodles and top with the lobster and the remaining spring onion greens. Serve with lime wedges and a side of the remaining sauce.

LEMONGRASS CHICKEN & RICE NOODLE SALAD

For the Lemongrass Chicken

2 pounds boneless skinless chicken thighs, cut into 2-inch cubes

3 tablespoons minced fresh ginger

2 tablespoons finely chopped lemongrass

2 tablespoons fish sauce

1 tablespoon sugar

1 medium garlic clove, peeled and minced

For the Salad

4 ounces rice vermicelli noodles

4 medium radishes, preferably an equal mix of watermelon and purple radishes, julienned (see page 70)

2 large carrots, peeled and julienned (see page 70)

1 medium seedless cucumber, julienned (see page 70)

2 cups packed fresh coriander leaves

2 cups packed fresh mint leaves

¼ cup roasted peanuts, roughly chopped

Tomato Nuoc Cham (see page 70), for serving

2 limes, sliced into wedges

Serves 4 to 6

This Vietnamese-inspired combination of savoury grilled meat and chilled rice noodle and herb salad has consistently been one of my most-requested dishes as a private chef, and I can see why. It's light, refreshing, and packed with flavour from the lemongrass marinade and nuoc cham, a high-acid, high-umami Vietnamese dipping sauce. This is the dish that made me fall in love with fish sauce, so if you're on the fence about it, this dish will convert you. Trust.

PREP THE CHICKEN: In a large zip-top bag, combine the chicken, ginger, lemongrass, fish sauce, sugar, and garlic. Close the bag and mix to combine the ingredients and coat the chicken. Marinate in the refrigerator for at least 30 minutes or up to overnight.

If using wooden skewers for your chicken, soak them in water for at least 30 minutes before grilling.

GRILL THE CHICKEN: Preheat the grill to medium-high.

Divide the chicken pieces among skewers, about 5 pieces per skewer. Grill, turning the skewers occasionally, until the chicken is charred and reaches an internal temp of 80°C, 10 to 15 minutes.

COOK THE NOODLES: Cook the noodles according to the package instructions. Drain and rinse under cold water, and set aside.

ASSEMBLE AND SERVE: In a large bowl, combine the noodles, radishes, carrots, cucumber, 1 cup each of the coriander and mint leaves, and 2 tablespoons of the peanuts. Drizzle with a few tablespoons of tomato nuoc cham and toss to mix.

Divide the salad among individual wide bowls. Top with equal portions of the skewered chicken per bowl and the remaining coriander, mint, and peanuts. Serve with nuoc cham and lime wedges.

HOT TIP

If you can't find fresh lemongrass, you can still make an equally delicious dish by substituting with an extra tablespoon of minced ginger.

grains

CRAB FRIED RICE

Prik Nam Pla Sauce

2 limes, juiced (about 3 tablespoons)

1 Thai chilli, finely chopped

1 tablespoon fish sauce

1 medium garlic clove, peeled and finely grated

For the Fried Rice

8 ounces white crabmeat

2 tablespoons unsalted butter

4 medium eggs, beaten

1 tablespoon fish sauce

1 tablespoon soy sauce

⅛ teaspoon sugar

2 tablespoons neutral cooking oil

4 medium garlic cloves, peeled and finely chopped

1 (2-inch) knob of ginger, peeled and finely chopped

5 cups cooked rice, preferably Thai jasmine (see Hot Tip)

1 bunch fresh coriander, leaves separated from stems and stems finely chopped

¾ cup chopped spring onions (white and green parts, about 4 spring onions)

4 mini cucumbers, thinly sliced

Lime wedges, for serving

Serves 4 to 6

HOT TIP

When making fried rice, it's best to use leftover, day-o d rice. Freshly cooked, the rice has too much moisture and will give you a mushy, clumpy result.

Of all the New York City neighborhoods I've lived in, NoLita is by far my favourite. My apartment was a mere two blocks from Uncle Boons, the best Thai restaurant in the city, and ordering crab fried rice (and the Khao Soi, page 88) was a standing weekly ritual. It was loaded with fresh coriander and spring onions, but the real star was the prik nam pla—the most perfect hit of lime juice-y brightness with chilli and garlic—that you'd drizzle over the top. Uncle Boons was one of the many restaurants that shut down for good during lockdown, so I had no choice but to teach myself how to make it.

MAKE THE PRIK NAM PLA SAUCE: In a small bowl, whisk together the lime juice, chilli, fish sauce, and grated garlic. Set aside.

PREP THE CRAB: Drain off any liquid in the container. Transfer the crabmeat to a cutting board or plate and comb through for any rogue pieces of shell and cartilage to discard. Transfer the cleaned crabmeat to a kitchen towel-lined plate and pat dry. Set aside.

SCRAMBLE THE EGGS: Heat a large high-sided carbon steel or nonstick frying pan over medium-low heat and add 1 tablespoon of butter. When the butter has melted, add the eggs and a teaspoon of water. Cook, stirring constantly with a rubber spatula, until they are fully cooked through, but still light and fluffy, 2 to 3 minutes. Transfer the eggs to a bowl and set aside. Wipe out any egg residue from the pan with a kitchen towel.

FRY THE RICE: In a small bowl, combine the fish sauce, soy sauce, and sugar and set aside.

Return the frying pan to medium-high heat and add the cooking oil and the remaining 1 tablespoon of butter. When the butter has melted, add the finely chopped garlic and ginger. Cook, stirring, until fragrant, about 1 minute, and then add the rice. Fry the rice, constantly stirring, until the garlic and ginger are incorporated and the rice is heated through, about 2 minutes. Add the fish sauce, soy sauce, and sugar, and toss to coat then fold in the coriander stems, half of the spring onions, and half of the crabmeat, taking care to not break up the big pieces of crab.

SERVE: Pile the rice high on a platter and top with the remaining crabmeat. Line the edges of the platter with sliced cucumber, coriander leaves, the remaining spring onions, and the lime wedges. Serve the prik nam pla sauce on the side.

FARRO BROCCOLI SALAD

2 cups apple cider or water

1 cup uncooked farro

4 sprigs fresh thyme

2 dried or fresh bay leaves

1 large head broccoli, cut into 1-inch florets

1 teaspoon garlic powder

¼ cup roasted pistachios

½ teaspoon fennel pollen or crushed fennel seeds

½ teaspoon crushed red pepper flakes

4 cups baby rocket or other tender greens

1 cup cherry tomatoes, halved

1 lemon, juiced (2 to 3 tablespoons)

1 cup packed fresh basil leaves, torn

1 cup shaved Parmesan cheese (about 3 ounces)

Extra-virgin olive oil

Kosher salt and flaky salt

Serves 4 to 6

Farro and I have history. During my brief stint in restaurant kitchens, I worked at a New York spot called Charlie Bird. Its farro salad was the star starter, and also the bane of my existence, since I had to make about one hundred of them each day. But if there was any preparation of this chewy, nutty, substantial grain that could withstand a rocky relationship, it's this one. Simmered in apple cider with earthy bay leaves—the Charlie Bird signature—it plumps up and takes on a subtle sweetness. The ingredients in the Charlie Bird farro salad rotated with the seasons but the formula was always 50 percent farro, 50 percent equal parts roasted veg, raw crunchy veg, toasted nuts, salty cheese, and fresh greens/herbs. The combination of ingredients below is catered to my personal preferences (it is MY cookbook, after all) but I encourage you to riff on the salad according to the seasons and YOUR personal preferences.

Preheat the oven to 220°C.

COOK THE FARRO: In a medium pot, combine the cider, farro, thyme, bay leaves, and 1 teaspoon of kosher salt with 1 cup of water. Bring to a boil, reduce to low, and cover. Simmer, stirring occasionally, until the farro is tender but not mushy, about 30 minutes. Drain any excess liquid, transfer the farro to a parchment paper-lined roasting tray, discarding the bay leaf and thyme, and spread the farro into an even layer to cool. To prevent it from clumping up, drizzle it with a touch of olive oil and toss to coat.

ROAST THE BROCCOLI: While the farro cooks, put the broccoli florets in a large bowl. Drizzle with enough olive oil to coat and season with garlic powder and a pinch of kosher salt. Spread the broccoli in an even layer over another roasting tray, leaving one-quarter of the tray empty. Roast for 15 minutes.

ROAST THE PISTACHIOS: Meanwhile, add the pistachios to the same bowl used for the broccoli and toss with the fennel pollen, pepper flakes, a pinch of kosher salt, and enough olive oil to coat.

Add the pistachios to the empty section of the roasting tray and return it to the oven. Bake until the nuts have toasted and the broccoli is tender and beginning to char in places, about 5 minutes more.

MAKE THE SALAD: Combine the farro, broccoli, pistachios, rocket, and tomatoes in a large bowl. Add the lemon juice, a drizzle of olive oil, and a good pinch of flaky salt and toss to combine. Just before serving, gently fold in the basil and Parm.

TOMATO AND SPOT PRAWN PAELLA

4 large ripe tomatoes, 2 of them chopped into 2-inch pieces and 2 of them whole

2 tablespoons finely chopped fresh flat-leaf parsley

½ lemon, zested and juiced (about 1 tablespoon), plus 2 lemons, sliced into wedges

1½ pounds peeled, deveined, head-on spot prawns or extra-large, head-on peeled, deveined prawns; shells reserved

1 medium shallot, peeled and finely chopped

2 medium garlic cloves, peeled and finely grated

1½ cups bomba rice or Arborio rice

¼ cup dry white wine, such as Pinot Grigio

1 teaspoon smoked paprika

1 teaspoon saffron threads

4 cups Shrimp Stock (recipe follows) or store-bought seafood stock

Extra-virgin olive oil

Kosher salt

Serves 4 to 6

HOT TIP

If you don't have a large oven-safe pan with a fitted lid, you can transfer the rice to a baking dish and cover it with kitchen foil.

When I studied abroad in Barcelona, I learned how to make traditional Spanish paella from a paella master. However, I am not a paella master and this is not traditional Spanish paella. After many failed attempts to re-create this dish back in the States, I could not, for the life of me, get it right. Instead of doubling down and investing in a fancy stovetop paella pan, like the one I borrowed from my food stylist for this photo, I stuck the whole thing in the oven and called it a day. I figured I'd throw in some nontraditional ingredients, too, such as white wine and marinated tomatoes. The result is a delicious seafood-studded rice dish that serves as the perfect centrepiece for a memorable meal. And that's what paella is all about, no?

Preheat the oven to 200°C.

MARINATE THE TOMATOES: In a small bowl, combine the diced tomatoes, 1 tablespoon olive oil, a pinch of salt, half of the chopped parsley, and the zest and juice from half of a lemon. Toss to coat.

SEAR THE PRAWNS: Heat a wide braising pan or frying pan over medium-high heat and add 1 tablespoon olive oil. Season the prawns with salt then, working in batches, sear the prawns until caramelized but still translucent in the centre, about 1 minute per side. Transfer seared prawns to a plate and set aside.

START THE PAELLA: To the same pan, add the shallot, garlic, and a pinch of salt and cook until softened, 3 minutes. Add the rice and cook, stirring constantly, until the rice is toasted, about 2 minutes. Deglaze with the white wine, scraping the pan.

Grate the whole tomatoes on a box grater and measure out about 1 cup of grated tomato. Once the wine has almost completely evaporated, add the tomato to the paella along with the paprika, saffron, and shrimp stock. Increase the heat to high and bring to a boil. Taste and season with salt.

CONTINUED

TOMATO AND SPOT PRAWN PAELLA

CONTINUED

BAKE THE PAELLA: Turn off the heat and cover the rice tightly with a lid. Transfer to the oven and bake for 15 minutes. Remove the lid and bake until the rice is tender and the liquid is almost fully absorbed, 10 to 15 minutes more. Nestle the prawns on top and bake until they are cooked through, 3 to 5 more minutes.

SERVE: Sprinkle the paella with the remaining parsley and then spoon the marinated tomatoes on top. Serve with extra lemon wedges.

SHRIMP STOCK

- 2 tablespoons unsalted butter
- 2 tablespoons extra-virgin olive oil
- Shells from 1½ pounds of prawns
- 3 medium carrots, chopped
- 3 celery stalks, chopped
- 1 medium yellow onion, peeled and chopped
- 1 small bulb of fennel, chopped
- 2 garlic cloves, peeled and crushed
- ½ cup tomato paste
- ¼ teaspoon kosher salt
- Freshly ground black pepper
- 1 cup dry white wine, such as Pinot Grigio

Makes about 8 cups

MAKE THE STOCK: Heat a large stock pot over medium heat and add the butter and olive oil. When the butter melts, add the prawn shells. Cook until the shells are fragrant and have infused the butter and oil with flavour, 3 to 5 minutes. If necessary, reduce the heat to medium-low to avoid browning or burning the shells.

Add the carrots, celery, onion, fennel, garlic, and tomato paste plus the salt and a few cracks of pepper. Cook, stirring occasionally, until the tomato paste starts to darken and caramelize, about 5 minutes.

Pour in the wine and stir with a wooden spoon, scraping up any brown bits from the bottom of the pan. Continue cooking until the wine reduces by about half, 3 minutes.

Add 8 cups cold water and bring it to a low boil. Reduce the heat to a simmer and cook, stirring occasionally, until the broth tastes rich and flavourful, about 1 hour. Turn off the heat and allow the stock to cool.

STRAIN THE STOCK: Place a large, fine-mesh sieve over a large bowl. Carefully ladle the stock, chunks and all, into the sieve. Use the back of the ladle to press down on the solids to squeeze out as much liquid as possible, then discard them.

USE OR STORE: If not using it now, divide the stock among airtight containers and store in the fridge for up to 3 days or in the freezer for up to 6 months.

MOM'S PILAF

1 tablespoon chicken bouillon

2 tablespoons unsalted butter

½ cup orzo pasta

1 medium shallot, peeled and finely chopped

2 medium garlic cloves, peeled and finely chopped

1 tablespoon fresh thyme leaves

¾ cup long-grain white rice, such as jasmine or basmati

1 tablespoon extra-virgin olive oil

1 tablespoon chopped fresh chives (optional)

Kosher salt

Serves 4 to 6

My mom's pilaf was unapologetically made from a box, and it was the gold standard. When I started cooking for myself, learning how to make this dish was high priority, and eventually I figured out how to recreate it from scratch. The secret ingredient? Chicken powder or chicken bouillon, which gives you that from-the-packet-flavour that chicken broth from a box, or even homemade for that matter, will never live up to (and we need to stop kidding ourselves that it ever could). It was, and still is, the ultimate fuss-free dish for when you don't have a lot of time to get dinner on the table.

PREP THE BROTH: In a medium bowl, whisk together the chicken bouillon and 2 cups of warm water. Set aside.

TOAST THE ORZO: Heat a medium saucepan over medium-high heat and add the butter. When the butter melts, add the orzo and cook, stirring occasionally, until it is lightly toasted and golden brown, about 5 minutes.

Add the shallot, garlic, and thyme plus a pinch of salt and cook until the shallot has softened, another 3 minutes. Stir in the rice and olive oil.

COOK THE PILAF: Add the bouillon broth and increase the heat to high. When it comes to a boil, reduce the heat to low, cover, and simmer until the rice and orzo are tender and the liquid absorbed, 20 to 25 minutes.

Turn off the heat and keep the pan covered for 5 minutes.

SERVE: Fluff the pilaf with a fork, season with salt, if needed, and fold in the chopped chives (if using).

HERBY RICE AND RADISH SALAD

1½ cups jasmine rice

1 cup packed fresh flat-leaf parsley leaves

½ cup packed fresh mint leaves

½ small shallot, peeled

¼ cup extra-virgin olive oil

2 lemons, zested and juiced (about ¼ cup)

3 cups microgreens or baby rocket

2 cups sugar snap peas or mange tout, sliced on the diagonal

1 bunch radishes, halved and thinly sliced

Kosher salt and flaky salt

Serves 4 to 6

Settling on sides when entertaining is often a thankless job. This herby rice salad has become my back-pocket carb for any and all occasions. She's dressed in a punchy herb sauce that pairs perfectly with practically everything. I sub her in during my most desperate menu moments, and she always delivers.

COOK THE RICE: Line a roasting tray with parchment paper and set aside.

Cook the rice according to the package instructions. Remove the pot from the heat and fluff the rice with a fork. Transfer the rice to the roasting tray, and spread it into an even layer to cool.

WHILE THE RICE COOKS, MAKE THE HERB OIL: In a blender or food processor, combine the parsley, mint, shallot, olive oil, and ½ teaspoon kosher salt. Blend or process until smooth. Set aside.

ASSEMBLE AND SERVE: Transfer the cooked rice to a large bowl, add the herb puree, lemon juice, lemon zest, and mix to combine. Gently fold in the microgreens, sugar snap peas, and radishes. Finish with flaky salt.

PECORINO POLENTA

½ stick (4 tablespoons) unsalted butter, plus more for preparing pan

1 cup stone-ground cornmeal polenta or grits

6 ounces freshly grated pecorino or Parmesan cheese (about 1½ cups), plus more for serving

Kosher salt and freshly ground black pepper

Serves 6 to 8

This recipe is adapted from my mom's formula for cheese grits, or buttery baked cornmeal loaded with cheese. And while I do enjoy the North Carolina breakfast delicacy, I much prefer the Italian approach to polenta. (Yes, grits and polenta are essentially the same thing; grits are polenta milled to a finer texture.) Sometimes you just need a sloppy, creamy pile of starch to pair with a saucy something, such as a braised short rib. This is that starch.

MAKE THE POLENTA: Preheat the oven to 180°C. Grease an 8-inch round baking dish or small cast-iron casserole dish with butter and set aside.

In a large saucepan, bring 4 cups of water and ½ teaspoon salt to a boil. Slowly whisk in the polenta, and then pour the mixture into the prepared baking dish. Cover with a lid or kitchen foil and bake for 45 minutes.

Remove from the oven, uncover, and stir in 1 cup of the cheese, the butter, and plenty of pepper. Taste and season with more salt, if needed. Sprinkle the top with the remaining ½ cup of cheese. Bake, uncovered, until the cheese is golden brown, about 15 minutes more.

SERVE: Spoon the polenta onto plates or into bowls and finish with more cheese and black pepper.

Store leftovers in an airtight container in the refrigerator for up to 3 days.

HOT TIP
For faster cooking, use "quick grits" or finely ground cornmeal polenta and reduce the baking time to 30 minutes.

surf

NANTUCKET CLAMBAKE

3 (1½-pound) lobsters

2 cups dry white wine, such as Pinot Grigio

1½ pounds baby red potatoes, halved

3 tablespoons chopped Calabrian chillies

5 cloves garlic, smashed

2 shallots, quartered

1 pound smoked fresh chorizo sausage, sliced on the diagonal into ½ inch pieces

24 littleneck clams, cleaned

1½ pounds shell-on king prawns (15 to 20), deveined

4 ears sweet corn, husks on

½ stick (4 tablespoons) salted butter

Chopped fresh flat-leaf parsley, for serving

Lemons, for serving

Grilled bread, for serving

Kosher salt

OPTIONAL ADDITIONAL DIPPING SAUCES: Melted Clarified Butter, Lemon Aïoli (page 43), Sesame Chilli Crunch (page 136), Tomato Nuoc Cham (page 70)

Serves 6

Inspired by your typical New England clambake, this version is much smaller, just like the teeny tiny island of Nantucket that stole my heart back in 1997. The objective: make a clambake using a standard 8-quart stock pot instead of a great big 16-quart lobster pot (because who's got the storage space for one of those anyways). To achieve this, I had to get creative with the limited space available. You'll notice mussels are MIA in this recipe, and that's because something had to go. If you feel strongly about adding them back in, be my guest, and good luck. For my next trick, I break down the lobsters BEFORE cooking them, because the inedible bodies consumed too much valuable real estate. And lastly, we're cooking the corn in the microwave because no one will know the difference. I told you we had to get creative here. Don't let all of these qualifiers scare you. While this may seem like one of the book's more challenging dishes, it's a deceptively simple, one-pot meal that comes together in under 45 minutes with very little active cooking time, and it makes for a hell of a fun dinner party.

PREP THE LOBSTERS: First, kill the lobsters. Working one at a time, place the tip of a large, sharp knife in the centre of a lobster's head, then swiftly insert the knife while bringing it down to be parallel with your cutting board. This is the most humane way to ready the lobsters for cooking.

Grab a clean tea towel to protect your hand and use a twist-and-pull motion to remove the tail and claws. Discard the bodies and legs, or use them for stock.

COOK THE CLAMBAKE: Place an 8-quart or larger stockpot or cast-iron casserole dish over high heat and add 2 cups of water, the wine, potatoes, Calabrian chillies, garlic, shallots, and 1 tablespoon of salt. Bring to a boil, cover, and cook for 6 minutes. Add the chorizo, clams, lobster tails, and lobster claws. Cover and cook until clams have opened and the lobsters are bright red, 8 to 10 minutes more. Add the prawns and cook until they are pink, opaque, and cooked through, 4 to 6 minutes more.

CONTINUED

NANTUCKET CLAMBAKE

CONTINUED

COOK THE CORN AND MELT THE BUTTER: With their husks on, microwave 1 to 2 ears of corn at a time on high power for 4 minutes. Cut off the stem end and remove the husk. Break the cobs in half and set aside until ready to serve with the rest of the clambake.

Add the butter to a medium saucepan and heat over medium until melted then turn off the heat and keep warm at the back of the stove.

ASSEMBLE: Preheat the oven to 90°C.

Using tongs, transfer the lobster, clams, potatoes, chorizo, and corn onto large platters or rimmed roasting trays. Discard any unopened clams. Cover tightly with kitchen foil and transfer to the oven to keep warm for up to 30 minutes. Strain the cooking liquid through a fine mesh sieve and add it to the melted butter. The broth will serve as the dip for your seafood boil, so taste and adjust the seasonings as you see fit. Whisk to combine and place over low heat until you're ready to serve.

TO SERVE: Set the table with lobster crackers and picks, buckets for collecting shells, and LOTS of napkins.

Remove the foil from the serving platters or trays and baste everything with a few spoons of the hot buttery broth and sprinkle with parsley. Portion the remaining broth into small bowls for each person. Arrange the platters in the centre of the table. Serve with lemon wedges, grilled bread for dipping, plus any additional sauces (it's fun to mix it up with these!).

TO EAT: Encourage guests to use their hands to serve themselves. Remove the lobsters, clams, and prawns from their shells, discard the shells into buckets, and eat the seafood as is, dipped in hot broth, clarified butter, or any sauce you'd like. Same goes for the potatoes, chorizo, and corn.

TOMATO BUTTER BAKED COD

½ stick (4 tablespoons) unsalted butter

1 tablespoon extra-virgin olive oil

1 small shallot, peeled and thinly sliced

3 medium garlic cloves, peeled and thinly sliced

1 tablespoon chopped Calabrian chillies

1 tablespoon tomato paste

2 cups cherry tomatoes, halved

1 cup dry white wine, such as Pinot Grigio, or juice of ½ lemon

4 to 6 (6- to 8-ounce) cod fillets

2 lemons, sliced into wedges, for serving

Fresh basil leaves, for serving

Kosher salt and freshly ground black pepper

Toasted bread, for serving

Serves 4 to 6

If you've been wanting to cook more fish at home but don't know where to start, look no further than this tomato cod that comes together in 30 minutes or less. Nestling the fish in a flavoursome buttery tomato sauce before slow roasting makes it both hands off and borderline foolproof. Feel free to swap with whatever flaky white fish you have available.

Preheat the oven to 190°C.

MAKE THE SAUCE: Heat a large ovenproof pan over medium heat and add the butter and olive oil. When the butter has melted, add the shallot, garlic, Calabrian chillies, and a pinch of salt. Cook, stirring, until fragrant, about 2 minutes. Add the tomato paste and continue to cook until it is lightly caramelized, about 2 minutes. Stir in 1½ cups of the cherry tomatoes and the wine. Simmer until the wine has reduced by half, about 5 minutes, smashing the tomatoes with your spoon to release their juices. Taste the sauce for salt and adjust as needed. Keep the sauce at a simmer. An optional step here is to blitz the sauce slightly with an immersion blender for a smoother consistency.

BAKE THE FISH: Season the cod with salt and nestle the fillets into the simmering sauce. Arrange the remaining ½ cup of tomatoes around the fish. Cover tightly with a lid and transfer the pan to the oven and bake until the fish is firm and flaky, 15 to 20 minutes.

SERVE: Finish with a squeeze of lemon and then top with basil. Serve directly from the pan with lemon wedges and toasted bread.

CHIVE CRAB CAKES

For the Crab Cakes

2 tablespoons unsalted butter

1 medium shallot, peeled and finely chopped

¾ cup plain flour

½ cup whole milk

2 tablespoons Dijon mustard

1 egg yolk

1 lemon, zested and sliced into wedges for squeezing

1 pound white crabmeat

2 tablespoons finely chopped fresh chives, plus more for serving

2 medium eggs, beaten

1¾ cups panko bread crumbs

Vegetable oil, as needed

Microgreens, for serving

Kosher salt

For the Lemon Beurre Blanc Sauce

2 sticks (16 tablespoons) unsalted butter, chilled and cubed into 16 pieces

1 medium shallot, peeled and finely chopped

⅓ cup dry white wine, such as Pinot Grigio

¼ cup Champagne vinegar

¼ cup double cream

1 lemon, zested and juiced (about 2 to 3 tablespoons)

Makes 6 crab cakes

Okay, confession: This is the most difficult recipe in the book. I went back and forth a hundred times about whether I should make it this extra, and you should know by now that I would never ask you to do more than absolutely necessary if it wasn't worth it. Well, these are worth it. Crab cakes are one of the many things in this life that I feel disproportionately passionate about, and the crab cake from Galley Beach Nantucket is my main muse. Perfection starts with a traditional French béchamel as the binder for the buttery, cloud-like suspension of crab that then is lightly coated with crispy panko, pan fried, and nestled in a pool of lemon beurre blanc sauce. I'm sorry, I don't make the rules. Consider this recipe your opportunity to cosplay as a culinary student for a day! Good luck!

MAKE THE BÉCHAMEL BINDER: Heat a medium saucepan over medium heat and add the butter. When the butter is melted, add the shallot and a pinch of salt. Cook, stirring, for about 1 minute. Whisk in 2 tablespoons of the flour and cook, whisking constantly, for about 1 minute.

Slowly whisk in the milk. Reduce the heat to low and cook, while whisking for another 2 minutes. Remove from the heat and transfer the mixture to a large bowl. Let cool to room temperature before whisking in the Dijon, egg yolk, about 1 teaspoon of lemon zest, and ¼ teaspoon of salt.

FORM THE CRAB CAKES: Add the crabmeat and chives to the butter mixture and stir gently, just until combined—you want a good combo of big and small chunks of crab. Taste (it's okay—nothing is raw in here) and season with salt. Form into 6 uniform cakes about 1 inch thick. Arrange on a roasting tray, cover with cling film, and transfer to the fridge to set for at least 4 hours, or overnight.

BREAD THE CRAB CAKES: Set up a dredging station with separate wide, shallow bowls for the remaining flour, the eggs, and the panko. Coat each crab cake in flour, then egg, then panko. Return the breaded crab cakes to the roasting tray and chill in the fridge so the breading can set, 15 to 30 minutes.

CONTINUED

CHIVE CRAB CAKES

CONTINUED

FRY THE CRAB CAKES: Preheat the oven to 90°C. Heat a large high-sided frying pan over medium-high heat and add ¼ inch of vegetable oil. When the oil is shimmering, add the crab cakes to the pan, working in batches, if necessary. Cook, flipping once, until the cakes are golden brown on both sides, about 4 minutes per side. Transfer the finished cakes to a wire rack-lined roasting tray to drain. Keep the cooked crab cakes warm in the oven for up to 30 minutes while you prepare the sauce.

MAKE THE LEMON BEURRE BLANC SAUCE: Heat a medium saucepan over medium heat and add 1 piece of the cold cubed butter. When the butter has melted, add the shallot. Cook, stirring several times, until the shallot has softened, about 1 minute.

Add the wine and vinegar and simmer until the liquid has almost completely evaporated, 1 to 2 minutes. Pour in the cream and heat the mixture to a simmer. Adjust the heat to medium-low and slowly whisk in the remaining butter, one piece at a time, waiting for each addition to fully melt and emulsify before adding the next piece.

When all of the butter has been incorporated and the sauce is emulsified, whisk in the lemon zest and lemon juice. The sauce should be thick enough to coat the back of a spoon. If the sauce splits at any point, reduce the heat to low and whisk in a few teaspoons of water and more cold butter until it comes back together. The sauce should be served immediately.

ASSEMBLE AND SERVE: Fill the base of shallow bowls with the lemon beurre blanc sauce. Place the crab cakes in the centre and top with microgreens and a squeeze of lemon.

HOT TIP

You can make the crab cakes a day in advance. Cook as directed then cool completely. Cover with kitchen foil or cling film and refrigerate overnight. Reheat at 220°C until they're crispy and warmed through, about 10 minutes.

SCAMPI SHRIMP

2 tablespoons extra-virgin olive oil, or more as needed

2 pounds shell-on king prawns (15 to 20), peeled and deveined

½ stick plus 1 tablespoon (5 tablespoons) unsalted butter, chilled and cut into 5 equal pieces

4 medium garlic cloves, peeled and finely chopped

2 Fresno chillies, stemmed, seeded, and finely chopped

1 small shallot, peeled and finely chopped

½ cup dry white wine, such as Pinot Grigio

Fresh basil leaves, for serving

2 lemons, zested and sliced into wedges, for serving

Crusty bread, for serving

Kosher salt

Serves 4 to 6

I'm not anti-shrimp scampi pasta, but these garlicky, butter-basted shrimp have truly met their match in the form of crusty bread, keeping the shrimp (and the butter) as the star.

SEAR THE PRAWNS: Heat a large high-sided frying pan over medium heat with 1 tablespoon of the olive oil. Working in batches, sear the prawns until caramelized on the outside but still translucent in the centre, about 1 to 2 minutes per side. Transfer the seared prawns to a plate and set aside.

MAKE THE BUTTER SAUCE: To the same pan, add 1 tablespoon of butter and the remaining 1 tablespoon of olive oil. When the butter has melted, add the garlic, chillies, shallot, and a pinch of salt. Cook, stirring once or twice, until fragrant, about 1 minute. Add the wine, stir up any bits from the bottom of the pan and cook until the wine is reduced by half, 3 to 4 minutes.

Adjust the heat to medium-low and whisk in the remaining 4 tablespoons of butter, one tablespoon at a time. When all the butter has been added, you should have a creamy, emulsified butter sauce.

Return the prawns to the pan. Toss to coat them with sauce and allow the prawns to finish cooking in the sauce while basting, 1 to 2 minutes.

SERVE: Plate the prawns, spoon over the sauce, and top with basil and the lemon zest. Serve with crusty bread and lemon wedges.

FISH TACOS

2 cups plain flour,
plus more for dusting

1 teaspoon baking powder

1 pound cod fillets, portioned into eight 2-ounce pieces

Vegetable oil, for frying

2 cups lager-style beer
(I like Modelo)

10 corn or flour tortillas

½ cup mayonnaise

1 lime, zested and juiced (about 1 tablespoon), plus 2 limes sliced into wedges, for serving

Pinch of chilli powder

½ a small head green cabbage, very finely shredded on a mandoline (about 3 cups)

Quick-Pickled Shallots (page 74), for serving

Thinly sliced jalapeño, for serving

Fresh coriander leaves, for serving

Hot sauce, for serving

Kosher salt, flaky salt, and freshly ground black pepper

Serves 4

This is my argument for frying fish at home. Is it a tiny bit fussier than throwing something in the oven? Almost certainly. Although, is it also literally the best thing I've made for myself? Without question. It just doesn't get more luxurious than treating yourself to the lightest, crispiest fish that demands instant inhalation in the form of a lime-y mayo-dressed taco, and I really want that for you. But if you're really not willing to do it, then I will confess that I've also made these with frozen fish sticks and they still hit.

Preheat the oven to 90°C.

FRY THE FISH: In a medium bowl, whisk together the flour, baking powder, and a pinch of salt. Set aside. Pat the fish dry with kitchen towel, season with salt and pepper and dust lightly with flour.

Fill a medium pot with enough oil to come 1½ inches up the sides. Heat over medium-high heat until the oil reaches 190°C.

Whisk the beer into the flour mixture just until incorporated. Do not overmix or the batter will lose its air and your fried fish won't be nice and crispy cloud-like.

When the oil is hot, dip the fish in the batter to fully coat. Allow excess batter to drip off before carefully lowering the pieces into the hot oil. Fry the fish in batches until crisp and golden on all sides, 3 to 5 minutes.

Use a slotted spoon or kitchen spider to transfer the fried fish to a wire rack-lined roasting tray to drain excess oil and season with flaky salt. Transfer the cooked fish to the oven to keep warm for up to 30 minutes.

WARM THE TORTILLAS: Over high heat on a gas stove, heat each tortilla directly over the flame until lightly charred, about 30 seconds per side. If you don't have a gas stove, heat a frying pan or griddle over high heat to warm the tortillas. Cook each about 30 seconds per side. Stack the tortillas on a plate and cover with a clean tea towel to keep them warm.

ASSEMBLE AND SERVE: In a small bowl, whisk together the mayo, lime zest, lime juice, and a pinch each of chilli powder, and salt. Place each piece of fish in a warm tortilla, drizzle with the mayo mixture, and top with cabbage, pickled shallots, jalapeño slices, and coriander. Serve with hot sauce, lots of lime wedges, and cold beer.

CRISPY FISH WITH CITRUS SALAD

For the Citrus Coriander Salsa Verde

½ cup packed fresh flat-leaf parsley leaves

½ cup packed fresh coriander leaves and stems

¼ cup extra-virgin olive oil

2 medium garlic cloves, peeled

½ a jalapeño

1 lemon, zested

½ teaspoon kosher salt

For the Citrus Salad and Fish

2 Cara Cara or navel oranges

1 grapefruit

5 mini cucumbers, halved lengthwise and sliced on the diagonal

2 medium avocados, pitted, peeled, and thinly sliced

½ cup Castelvetrano olives, pitted and roughly chopped

1 medium shallot, peeled and thinly sliced

½ of a jalapeño, thinly sliced

4 to 6 (6- to 8-ounce) skin-on Chilean sea bass fillets

Plain flour (optional)

1 lemon, halved, for serving

Extra-virgin olive oil

Kosher salt, flaky salt, and freshly ground black pepper

Serves 4 to 6

This is my favourite back-pocket fish recipe. It's bright and fresh and doesn't require any pro chef moves other than crisping up the fish in a pan, slathering it in an herb puree, and throwing together a citrusy salsa with avocado and olives. Chilean sea bass is used here but any white fish would work, or even salmon!

Preheat the oven to 90°C.

MAKE THE CITRUS CORIANDER SALSA VERDE: Use an immersion blender to blend the parsley, coriander, olive oil, garlic, jalapeño, lemon zest, and kosher salt until smooth. Alternatively you can hand chop, or use a food processor.

MAKE THE CITRUS SALAD: Slice the ends off the oranges and grapefruit. Run a paring knife around the edge of the citrus to remove the peel and the white pith. Then use the knife to slice between the membranes to remove the segments. (Congrats, you just supremed.)

Squeeze the juice from the cores/membranes of the oranges and grapefruit into a medium bowl. Add the orange and grapefruit supremes, the cucumbers, avocados, olives, shallot, jalapeño slices, 1 tablespoon of olive oil, and a pinch of flaky salt. Toss to combine and set aside.

COOK THE FISH: Pat the fillets dry with a kitchen towel and season the flesh side with salt. For extra-crispy skin (if desired), dust the skin with a light coating of flour.

Place a stainless steel or nonstick frying pan over medium heat. When it's hot, add 2 tablespoons of olive oil and heat the oil until it shimmers.

Working in batches, sear the fish skin side down while applying light pressure with a spatula to the centre of the fillets to ensure even contact with the pan. Cook on the first side until the flesh is opaque two-thirds of the way up the side of the fish, 4 to 6 minutes. Flip, season the skin with salt, and cook for another 1 to 2 minutes.

Cook the remaining fillets, adding more oil to the pan as needed. The cooked fish can be kept warm in the oven for up to 15 minutes.

ASSEMBLE AND SERVE: Spoon some of the citrus coriander salsa verde on each plate. Pile the citrus salad on one side, plate the fish on the other, and hit each fillet with a squeeze of lemon juice.

BUTTERFLIED BRANZINO

For the Red Chilli Sauce

2 tablespoons chopped Calabrian chillies

2 tablespoons extra-virgin olive oil

1 lemon, zested and juiced (2 to 3 tablespoons)

1 garlic clove, peeled

¼ teaspoon kosher salt

For the Parsley Caper Salsa Verde

1 cup fresh flat-leaf parsley leaves

¼ cup extra-virgin olive oil

2 tablespoons capers in brine, drained

1 garlic clove, peeled

¼ teaspoon kosher salt

For the Fish

4 (1½-pound) branzino, butterflied and deboned, head and tail left on (ask your fishmonger)

Extra-virgin olive oil

4 lemons, sliced, plus 2 lemons, cut into wedges, for serving

Kosher salt and freshly ground black pepper

Serves 4

HOT TIP

If you can't find branzino, you can use any fish you'd like although I recommend 2 (2- to 3-pound) sea bass or red snappers.

My mom's favourite dish to order in restaurants is branzino, roasted whole and typically stuffed with lemons and herbs. I started making it for her at home during lockdown with my own very predictable spin of adding a citrusy salsa verde to the mix. Fast forward to a trip I took to Mexico City where I had the pleasure of dining at Contramar and having its famous Green and Red Fish, a whole grilled snapper basted with green herb sauce and red chilli sauce—with the white-fleshed fish, it's a playful nod to the colours of the Mexican flag. Since the Italian flag is also green, white, and red, it felt right to make those sauces Italian style. If you're not yet up to cooking a whole fish, you can easily make this using branzino fillets.

Set the top rack in your oven 5 inches from the grill and preheat the grill on high.

MAKE THE RED CHILLI SAUCE: Use an immersion blender to blend the Calabrian chillies, olive oil, lemon zest and juice, garlic, and salt until smooth. Alternatively you can hand chop.

MAKE THE PARSLEY CAPER SALSA VERDE: Use an immersion blender to blend the parsley, olive oil, capers, garlic, and salt until smooth. Alternatively you can hand chop.

COOK THE FISH: Line a roasting tray with kitchen foil and a wire rack. Brush the wire rack with olive oil and arrange a layer of sliced lemons for the fish to lie on. This will prevent the delicate flesh from sticking to the wire rack, flavour the fish, and help to keep it moist.

Coat the fish with olive oil and season with salt and pepper inside and out.

Open the fish and lay each one, skin side up, over the lemons. Spoon chilli sauce over one side and salsa verde over the other. Grill until the skin is slightly charred and the fish is flaky, 5 to 7 minutes for branzino and 8 to 12 minutes for larger fish.

At this point there are still a few pin bones attached to the branzino fillets. These can easily be removed now that the fish is fully cooked, or I usually opt to just eat around them. Just be sure to give your guests a heads up.

SERVE: Plate the fish crispy skin side-up. Serve with lemon wedges.

SLOW-ROASTED SALMON WITH PONZU AND SESAME CHILLI CRUNCH

1 (2½-pound) skin-on salmon fillet

2 lemons, thinly sliced

2 limes, thinly sliced

Sesame Chilli Crunch (page 136), for serving or store-bought chilli crisp

Ponzu, for serving

¾ cup diagonally sliced spring onions (white and green parts, about 4 spring onions)

Cooked sushi rice for serving

4 mini cucumbers, sliced, for serving

2 avocados, sliced, for serving

Extra-virgin olive oil

Kosher salt

Serves 4 to 6

If you're like me, then you experience very intense and unignorable cravings for sushi on a weekly basis. This dish is my answer to those cravings. What I realized is that I don't really need sushi-sushi to scratch this itch—just fish, rice, and the citrusy, Japanese ponzu sauce. Salmon that's slow-roasted but still very pink in the centre is not a consolation prize—it's the real deal. Especially when it's doused with a chunky, sesame-studded, dried chilli-packed, oily, vinegary drizzle that's somewhere between Chinese chilli crisp and Mexican salsa macha.

Preheat the oven to 140°C.

SLOW ROAST THE SALMON: Using a sharp knife, make a few small incisions into the salmon skin without slicing into the flesh. Season both sides of the salmon with salt. Drizzle 1 tablespoon of olive oil on a small roasting tray and arrange the lemon and lime slices in an even layer on the pan. Place the fish, skin side down, on top of the citrus slices. The citrus will prevent the fish from sticking to the pan, help retain its moisture, and flavour it as it cooks. Bake until the salmon is flaky but still slightly pink on the inside, 30 to 35 minutes.

While the salmon is roasting, make the sesame chilli crunch.

ASSEMBLE AND SERVE: Transfer the salmon to a platter and top with a few tablespoons of ponzu, a few spoonfuls of the sesame chilli crunch, and some of the thinly sliced spring onions. Serve with rice, sliced cucumber, avocado, more ponzu, more spring onions, and more sesame chilli crunch.

turf

NOT MY MOM'S ROAST CHICKEN

1 (3- to 4-pound) whole chicken

2 tablespoons extra-virgin olive oil

2 tablespoons unsalted butter

1 pound Yukon Gold potatoes, halved

3 large carrots, left whole or cut into 2-inch pieces

4 to 5 large shallots, halved or quartered, roots left intact, and peeled

5 medium garlic cloves, smashed and peeled

1 cup dry white wine, such as Pinot Grigio, or chicken stock

5 sprigs fresh thyme

1 lemon, thinly sliced

Kosher salt, flaky salt, and freshly ground black pepper

For the Parsley Tarragon Salsa Verde

1 cup fresh flat-leaf parsley leaves

¼ cup fresh tarragon

¼ cup extra-virgin olive oil

1 tablespoon Dijon mustard

2 garlic cloves

¼ teaspoon kosher salt

Serves 4 to 6

As the name indicates, this dish is inspired by my mom's roast chicken recipe, also known as the chicken that started it all—the wishbone behind Wishbone Kitchen. While carving the roast chicken, my mom always saved us the wishbone, then after dinner we'd each hold on to a half, make a wish, and pull. And while the core memory for me is snapping bones in half to see whose hopes and dreams would get to come true, the chicken itself is a standout. Unlike the bronzed bird you usually think of when you hear "roast chicken," this version cooks in a covered cast-iron casserole dish over a bed of carrots and potatoes so it doesn't so much roast as it steams while all those juices infuse into the veg. The beauty of cooking chicken this way is that you're not stressing about nailing that perfect golden crust because it's beside the point when you can have perfectly moist, flavourful meat and a one-pot meal. What makes this NOT my mom's roast chicken is the addition of wine, butter, and a generous basting of garlicky herb sauce.

Preheat the oven to 200°C.

PREP THE CHICKEN: Remove the chicken from the fridge and from its packaging and allow it to sit at room temperature for about 1 hour before roasting. This will allow for more even cooking.

SEAR THE CHICKEN: Pat dry the chicken with kitchen towels and season inside and out with 3 to 4 teaspoons of salt (see Hot Tip).

Heat a large cast-iron casserole dish over medium-high heat and add the olive oil. When the oil shimmers, add the chicken breast side down and sear until golden brown, about 5 minutes. Use tongs to carefully turn the chicken on its side to sear the legs and thighs, about 5 minutes per side. Transfer the chicken to a plate and set aside.

SAUTÉ THE VEG: Add the butter to the pan along with the potatoes, carrots, shallots, garlic, a pinch of kosher salt, and a few cracks of pepper. Cook, stirring occasionally, until fragrant, about 3 minutes. Pour in the wine and use a wooden spoon to scrape up any browned bits from the bottom of the pan. Allow the wine to cook down and reduce by half, 3 to 5 minutes.

CONTINUED

NOT MY MOM'S ROAST CHICKEN

CONTINUED

Scatter the thyme and lemon slices over the vegetables. Nestle the chicken on top of the vegetables, breast side up. Cover with a lid and transfer to the oven.

ROAST THE CHICKEN AND VEG: Roast until the internal temperature reaches 80°C in the meatiest part of the thigh, 60 to 90 minutes.

MAKE THE PARSLEY TARRAGON SALSA VERDE: Use an immersion blender or food processor to blend the parsley, tarragon, olive oil, mustard, garlic, and salt until smooth. Alternatively, finely chop the ingredients by hand.

CARVE THE CHICKEN: Transfer the chicken to a cutting board and allow it to rest for 30 minutes before carving. Carve the chicken according to the instructions on page 201. Brush the chicken pieces with the parsley tarragon salsa verde. Slice the breasts into ½- to 1-inch slices for serving.

SERVE: Transfer the vegetables to plates or a serving bowl and season with flaky salt and a couple cracks of pepper. Arrange the chicken over the top and finish with more salsa verde.

HOT TIP

A general rule of thumb is to season meat with about ½ teaspoon of salt per pound of meat. Seasoning with salt hours in advance of cooking, preferably the night before, allows enough time for the salt to fully penetrate into the meat. Otherwise, it's best to season minutes if not seconds before searing, since the salt will eventually draw moisture to the surface of the meat and prevent browning.

HOT TIP

You can also prepare this with 4 bone-in, skin-on chicken breasts. Just reduce the roasting time to 30 to 45 minutes.

how to carve a chicken

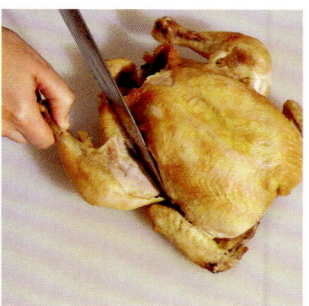
Pull the legs away from the body and slice through the skin to expose the hip joint.

Use your hands to dislocate the joint and slice through to remove the leg from the body.

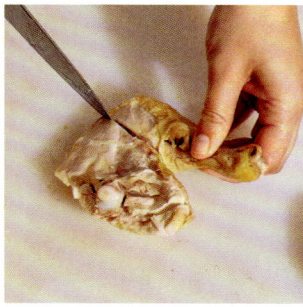
Find where the drum meets the thigh—there will be a faint line separating the two muscle groups. Cut along that line to expose the joint.

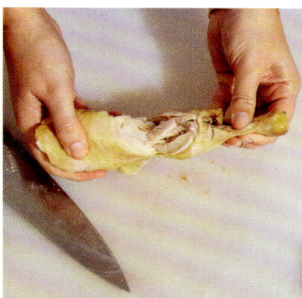
Dislocate the joint.

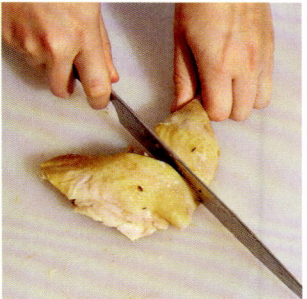
Slice all the way through. Repeat with the other leg.

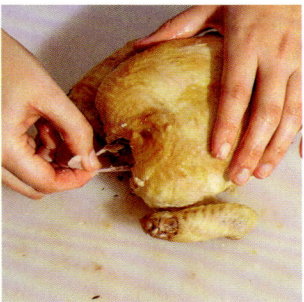
Before carving the breast, locate the wishbone within the top of the breasts connected to the breast bone.

In a tender chicken, you can usually wiggle it loose and remove it by hand. Otherwise, use a pairing knife to carve it out.

Locate the hard breast bone down the centre of the chicken separating the breasts. Position your knife directly beside it and slice down along the breast bone until you reach the ribcage.

Position your knife at an angle while you carve off the breast meat, keeping the knife as close to the ribcage as possible, peeling back the breast meat as you carve so you can see where you're slicing.

Repeat with the other breast.

Slice around the armpit of the chicken wings to expose the joint, dislocate the joint, and slice through.

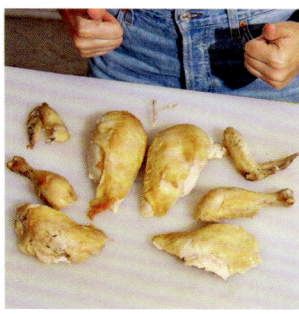
Congrats, you've just carved a chicken!

TURF

SHAKE 'N BAKE CHICKEN WITH HOT HONEY TOMATOES

1 medium egg, beaten

¼ cup mayonnaise

2 tablespoons Dijon mustard

2 pounds boneless, skinless chicken thighs

2 cups panko bread crumbs

2 teaspoons garlic powder

1 teaspoon smoked paprika

Pinch of cayenne pepper

3 tablespoons hot honey, plus more for serving

2 tablespoons chilli-infused olive oil, or extra-virgin olive oil with a pinch of crushed red pepper flakes

1 lemon, zested and juiced (about 3 tablespoons)

2 cups cherry tomatoes, halved

2 tablespoons finely chopped fresh chives

6 cups packed baby rocket

2 ounces freshly shaved Parmesan cheese

Kosher salt, flaky salt, and freshly ground black pepper

Serves 4

While my mom was (is) a fantastic from-scratch cook, she was never too good for a kitchen short cut, Shake 'N Bake being a prime example. This ingenious breading method has you skip the chaos and the mess of a traditional dredging station by containing it all in a plastic zip-top bag. So all you do is shake, and bake! Honestly, iconic. This recipe has the same mess-free ethos, with the addition of a pre-panko step that coats the chicken in mayo and Dijon for maximum flavour and juiciness. (But don't worry this step is also contained to a bag.) Served with a simple side of rocket and spicy yet sweet marinated tomatoes, it's as weeknight as weeknight gets.

Preheat the oven to 220°C.

SHAKE THE CHICKEN: In a large zip-top bag, combine the egg, mayo, mustard, ½ teaspoon salt, and a couple cracks of pepper. Add the chicken to the bag and tightly zip it closed. Working through the bag, massage the chicken with your hands to fully coat it.

In a second large zip-top bag, combine the panko, garlic powder, paprika, cayenne pepper, and ½ teaspoon salt. Working with one piece at a time, add the chicken from the first bag to the second bag with the panko mixture, seal the bag, and gently shake the bag to coat the chicken with the crumb mixture. Transfer the chicken to a wire rack-lined roasting tray and repeat with the remaining pieces.

BAKE THE CHICKEN: Bake until the chicken is golden brown and the internal temperature reaches 80°C, 25 to 30 minutes.

MARINATE THE TOMATOES: In a medium bowl, whisk together the hot honey, chilli-infused oil, half of the lemon zest, and 2 tablespoons of the lemon juice. Add the tomatoes, chives, and a pinch of flaky salt and toss to coat. Set aside.

ASSEMBLE AND SERVE: When still hot from the oven, drizzle the chicken with hot honey and sprinkle with flaky salt. Dress the rocket with the remaining 1 tablespoon of lemon juice, remaining lemon zest, a pinch of salt, and a couple cracks of pepper. Toss to coat. Gently fold in the shaved Parm. Plate the rocket and the chicken and top with the marinated tomatoes plus any remaining marinade from the bowl.

BOYFRIEND ROAST CHICKEN WITH PAN-SAUCE POTATOES

1 (4-pound) whole chicken

1 tablespoon Espelette pepper, or sweet paprika

2 teaspoons dried oregano

2 teaspoons garlic powder

½ stick (4 tablespoons) salted butter, melted

1 pound baby Yukon gold potatoes

½ a large shallot, peeled and finely chopped

1 tablespoon Champagne vinegar or white wine vinegar

1 tablespoon wholegrain or Dijon mustard

2 tablespoons finely chopped chives, plus more for serving

Kosher salt and freshly ground black pepper

Serves 4

HOT TIP

Salting the chicken overnight allows the salt to fully penetrate the meat while simultaneously drying out the skin, which delivers a golden, crispy exterior and a flavourful juicy exterior.

This is my personal favourite way to roast a chicken, especially for guests that I'm desperate to impress (a feeling that I'm all too familiar with, particularly in those first few months into a new relationship, during which this recipe was born). No, I am not telling you to channel your inner 1950s housewife and roast a chicken just to impress a potential suitor but I'm also not going to tell you that it doesn't work. Does the beauty prep start the day before? Yes. Does she take two hours to get ready the night of? Also yes. But same . . . and the results speak for themselves.

PREP THE CHICKEN: Pat the chicken dry with kitchen towels. Season the chicken inside and out with 3 to 4 teaspoons salt. Place the chicken, breast side up, on a wire rack-lined roasting tray and refrigerate, uncovered, overnight.

Preheat the oven to 200°C.

Remove the chicken from the fridge and let it stand at room temperature for 1 hour, then pat dry again with kitchen towels.

SEASON THE CHICKEN: In a medium bowl, mix together the Espelette pepper, oregano, garlic powder, lots of freshly ground black pepper, and just a tiny pinch of salt (since we salted the bird already). Brush the entire outside of the chicken with melted butter, then coat in the seasoning mixture, being sure to get in all of the nooks and crannies.

TRUSS THE CHICKEN: Grab on to the end of each leg and cross one over the other at the ankles. Wrap butcher's twine around the ankles several times, then tie tightly to secure them. This process allows the chicken to cook more evenly but if you don't have twine, you can skip this step. Tuck the wing tips behind the shoulders to prevent them from burning.

CONTINUED

BOYFRIEND ROAST CHICKEN WITH PAN-SAUCE POTATOES

CONTINUED

ROAST THE CHICKEN: Preheat a large cast-iron frying pan over medium-high heat. When the pan is hot, add the chicken to the pan, breast side up. Turn off the stove and carefully transfer the pan to the oven, placing it on a lower middle rack. As an optional but recommended step, place a large roasting tray directly below on the very bottom rack to catch any rogue chicken juices. Roast until the internal temperature reaches 80°C in the meatiest part of the thigh, 60 to 90 minutes.

BOIL THE POTATOES: Add the potatoes to a large pot and cover with cold water. Liberally season with salt and bring to a boil. Reduce to a simmer and cook until the potatoes are fork tender, 15 to 20 minutes. Drain the potatoes. Once the potatoes have slightly cooled but are still warm, gently crush them in your hand to break the skin and expose the flesh. Transfer the crushed potatoes to a large mixing bowl and cover with foil to keep warm.

MAKE THE PAN SAUCE: When the chicken is done roasting, remove the pan from the oven and carefully transfer the chicken to a cutting board, leaving behind all of the pan drippings and juices in the pan. Allow the chicken to rest for 30 minutes before carving.

There should be about ⅓ cup of drippings left in the pan. If not, supplement with a few tablespoons of melted butter. While the pan is still hot, whisk in the shallot, vinegar, and mustard.

FINISH THE POTATOES: Pour about half of the pan sauce over the hot crushed potatoes along with the chives and mix to combine. Taste for salt and pepper and season accordingly. Cover with kitchen foil to keep warm and set aside.

SERVE: Carve the chicken according to the instructions on page 201, slice the breast into ½- to 1-inch slices, and arrange the pieces on a platter. Spoon over the remaining pan sauce. Garnish the potatoes with more chives and serve.

DUCK LETTUCE WRAPS

For the Duck Confit Larb

¼ cup kosher salt

4 duck legs

1 pound duck fat

1 cup loosely packed fresh mint leaves

1 cup loosely packed fresh coriander leaves

1 shallot, peeled and thinly sliced

1 tablespoon fish sauce

1 tablespoon lime juice

1 tablespoon chilli flakes

½ tablespoon toasted rice powder (see Hot Tip)

Cooked white rice, preferably jasmine, for serving

For the Duck Lettuce Wraps

2 boneless, skin-on duck breasts

2 heads Bibb lettuce, leaves separated

1 medium carrot, julienned (page 70)

4 mini cucumbers, julienned (page 70)

4 limes, sliced into wedges

1 cup loosely packed fresh mint leaves

1 cup loosely packed fresh coriander leaves

1 shallot, thinly sliced

Tomato Nuoc Cham (page 70), for serving

Kosher salt

Serves 4 to 6

This Thai-larb-meets-Vietnamese-lettuce-wrap dish was actually inspired by my, and my family's, favourite dish at The Nautilus Nantucket. The dish was a roasted Peking duck with steamed bao buns, lettuce wraps, fresh herbs, and sauces for DIY assembling. I vividly remember the first time my family and I ordered a dish that was designed to be shared. This was more than a decade ago—dining experiences like this are extremely common these days—but it struck me at the time as revolutionary. We were like little kids on Christmas morning, making our little buns and wrapping little wraps. It was a truly joyful experience and one that has always stuck with me. The structure of this dish is sort of similar, but instead of going the roasted Peking duck route, we're cooking the breast and legs separately. The duck breasts are simply seared until medium-rare then topped with my favourite nuoc cham for Vietnamese-inspired lettuce wraps, while the duck legs confit, shredded then tossed with fresh herbs and fish sauce, reminiscent of a Thai larb. They can be enjoyed separately, but together they make for a hell of a dinner party centrepiece.

CURE THE DUCK LEGS: Massage ¼ cup of kosher salt into the duck legs. Transfer to a container, cover with cling film, and refrigerate overnight.

Preheat the oven to 140°C.

CONFIT THE DUCK: Under cold running water, rinse the excess salt from the duck legs. Pat them dry with kitchen towels and set aside.

In a large cast-iron casserole dish over medium heat, melt the duck fat. Turn off the heat.

Add the duck legs, skin side-up, making sure they're completely submerged in fat. Cover and bake until the meat is tender and falling off the bone, 4 to 5 hours. Remove from the oven, and let the duck sit in the pot for 30 minutes before transferring to a cutting board. Reserve 2 tablespoons of the duck fat to use in the recipe and store the rest in an airtight container in the fridge for up to 6 months.

SHRED THE DUCK CONFIT: Carefully remove the skin and set aside. (We'll use this later.) Using your hands, pull the meat from the bones and shred it. Transfer the shredded meat to a bowl and cover with kitchen foil to keep warm.

CONTINUED

DUCK LETTUCE WRAPS

CONTINUED

CRISP THE CONFIT SKIN: Heat a large stainless steel frying pan over medium-high heat and add 2 tablespoons of reserved duck fat. When the fat shimmers, add the duck skin. Fry until golden brown and crispy, about 5 minutes per side. Transfer to a kitchen towel-lined plate to cool.

COOK THE DUCK BREASTS: Score the skin with a sharp knife and season both sides with salt. Place both breasts in a cold stainless steel pan, skin side down, and set over medium-low heat. Slowly render out the fat for about 10 minutes. Increase the heat to medium-high and continue cooking on the skin side until golden brown and then flip the breasts. Cook on the second side until the internal temperature reaches 60°C, about 4 minutes. Remove from the pan and set aside to rest 10 to 15 minutes before slicing.

ASSEMBLE: In a large mixing bowl, combine the shredded duck confit, with the mint, coriander, shallot, fish sauce, lime juice, chilli flakes, and toasted rice powder. Toss to combine.

Thinly slice the duck breast on the bias.

SERVE: Arrange the duck confit mixture and sliced duck breast on a serving platter. Serve with large lettuce leaves for wrapping, the crispy duck skin, carrots, cucumbers, lime wedges, the remaining coriander and mint, and rice plus nuoc cham for dipping.

TO EAT: Eat the duck confit larb with rice or in a lettuce wrap with added veg and herbs plus a squeeze of lime. For the breast, add to a lettuce wrap with veg and herbs and drizzle with nuoc cham. Feel free to mix and match!

HOT TIP
To make your own toasted rice powder, toast 2 tablespoons of uncooked jasmine rice in a dry sauté pan over medium heat until deeply golden brown. Let cool, then grind into a powder using a spice grinder or a mortar and pestle.

PORK TACOS WITH ROASTED PEACH SALSA

1 (6- to 8-pound) bone-in pork shoulder

½ cup kosher salt

½ cup packed light brown sugar

3 tablespoons apple cider vinegar

Corn tortillas, for serving

Roasted Peach Salsa (recipe follows), for serving

Tomatillo Salsa Verde (recipe follows), for serving

4 ripe peaches, finely chopped, for serving

1 medium white onion, finely chopped, for serving

Fresh coriander leaves and stems, finely chopped, for serving

4 limes sliced into wedges, for serving

Serves 10

HOT TIP

This recipe will yield a lot of pork, but it freezes and reheats really well. After shredding, allow the meat to fully cool before transferring to a freezer-safe container. Freeze for up to 6 months. Alternatively, sub for a smaller, boneless pork shoulder roast. Just reduce the cooking time accordingly.

Somewhere between my mom's North Carolina-style pulled pork and my favourite Mexico City street tacos live these pork tacos with peach salsa. I've traded the traditional preparation of pork carnitas, simmering large pieces of pork in rendered pork fat on the stove, for Carolina-ish-style oven-roasted pork. My motivation? Less active cooking time (and less pork fat) necessary. Now if you're like my dad and have an affinity for smoking meats, you can throw the pork butt on a smoker at 120°C for 8 hours for extra credit. I figured while we're bringing these two beautiful culinary universes together, why not seal the deal with a southern peach salsa? It's sweet, it's spicy, and it pairs perfectly with the roast pork. I've also included a tomatillo salsa verde for a more traditional street taco flavour experience.

Preheat the oven to 150°C.

ROAST THE PORK: Remove the pork from the fridge and let it sit at room temperature for 1 hour before cooking. In a small bowl, stir together the salt and brown sugar. Coat the entire outside of the pork with the mixture. Transfer the meat to a roasting tray lined with kitchen foil and a wire rack. Cover tightly with foil, crimping and sealing tightly along the base of the roasting tray. Bake for 3 hours, then remove the foil and continue to bake, uncovered, until the pork is fall-apart tender, 3 to 4 hours more. Transfer the pork to a cutting board, cover with foil, and allow it to rest for 1 hour.

SHRED THE PORK: I find that the best method for shredding pork is with your hands. The meat can still be really hot on the inside so wear one or two layers of food-safe gloves. Alternatively, use metal tongs or two large forks for shredding. Transfer the shredded pork to a large bowl along with the vinegar (this will keep the meat moist) and ½ teaspoon of salt. Cover tightly with foil to keep warm and prevent the steam from escaping and the meat from drying out.

HEAT THE TORTILLAS: Over high heat on a gas stove, heat each tortilla directly over the flame until partially charred, about 30 seconds per side. If you don't have a gas stove, heat a frying pan or griddle pan over high heat and warm each tortilla in the pan, 30 seconds per side. Stack the tortillas on a plate and cover with a clean tea towel to keep warm. If needed, microwave the tortillas on the towel-covered plate for 15 to 30 seconds right before serving.

CONTINUED

PORK TACOS WITH ROASTED PEACH SALSA

CONTINUED

CRISP THE PORK: This step is optional but will give you extra-crispy bits reminiscent of traditional carnitas. Preheat your grill to high. Working in batches, arrange the pork in an even layer on a foil-lined roasting tray. Just before serving, pop the tray under the grill for 2 to 5 minutes until pork is crispy and heated through.

SERVE: Serve the pork with the warm tortillas, peach salsa, tomatillo salsa verde, diced peaches, diced onion, coriander, and lime wedges.

BUILD YOUR TACO: I like building one classic style with just pork, salsa verde, diced onion, fresh coriander, and a squeeze of lime. Then another with the peach salsa, diced peaches, diced onion, coriander, and a squeeze of lime.

ROASTED PEACH SALSA

4 ripe, skin-on peaches, halved and pitted

¼ teaspoon light brown sugar

½ habanero pepper or serrano pepper

¼ white onion, peeled and roughly chopped

¼ cup tightly packed coriander leaves and stems, roughly chopped

Zest and juice of 1 lime (2 tablespoons of juice)

1 teaspoon apple cider vinegar

½ teaspoon kosher salt

Preheat the oven to 150°C.

ROAST THE PEACHES: The peaches bake at the same temperature as the pork, so you can add them to the oven along with the meat or bake ahead of time. Arrange the peaches, cut side up, in a single layer on a roasting tray and sprinkle with brown sugar. Transfer to the oven and bake until softened, about 1½ hours. When the peaches are done roasting, allow them to cool for 30 minutes before blending.

MAKE THE PEACH SALSA: Transfer the cooled peaches to a blender or food processor along with the habanero pepper, onion, coriander, lime zest, lime juice, apple cider vinegar, and salt. Pulse until combined for a slightly chunky consistency. Transfer to the fridge to chill before serving.

PORK TACOS WITH ROASTED PEACH SALSA

CONTINUED

TOMATILLO SALSA VERDE

6 tomatillos (see Hot Tip), papery husks removed

5 medium jalapeños

½ small white onion, peeled

5 garlic cloves, peeled

1 bunch fresh coriander, leaves and stems roughly chopped (about 1½ cups)

1 teaspoon kosher salt

BOIL THE TOMATILLOS: Bring a large pot of water to a boil. Add the tomatillos, jalapeños, onion, and garlic. Reduce the heat to medium-low and simmer until the veg have softened, 7 to 10 minutes. Use a slotted spoon to transfer the veg to a bowl and set aside to cool. Reserve about 1 cup of the cooking water.

MAKE THE TOMATILLO SALSA: Once cool, transfer the veg mixture to a blender or food processor along with the coriander and salt. Blend until smooth, adding a few splashes of the reserved cooking water as needed to adjust the texture. Taste and adjust the salt. Transfer to the fridge to chill before serving.

HOT TIP

If you can't find tomatillos, you can sub in green tomatoes for a similar result. Or you can use regular tomatoes, which will taste similar but obviously not give you that salsa verde green hue.

HARISSA PITAS WITH FETA AND CUCUMBER

For the Pitas

1 tablespoon extra-virgin olive oil

2 pounds meat mince (I like using a mix of lamb and beef)

2 tablespoons Harissa Seasoning Blend (page 112) or store-bought

½ cup harissa sauce

2 tablespoons tomato paste

4 medium garlic cloves, peeled and finely grated

8 pita bread, for serving

Baby rocket or watercress

Kosher salt and freshly ground black pepper

For the Feta Dressing

4 ounces feta cheese in brine, plus more for serving

1 cup plain whole-milk Greek yogurt

1 medium garlic clove, peeled and finely grated

1 lemon, zested and sliced into wedges

Kosher salt and freshly ground black pepper

For the Cucumber Salad

1 large Persian cucumber, diced small

1 medium shallot, peeled and finely chopped

½ cup fresh flat-leaf parsley leaves, roughly chopped

¼ cup fresh mint leaves, roughly chopped

Juice of ½ lemon

Kosher salt

Serves 4

The convenience of beef mince taco night meets the deliciousness of a halal cart pita for this big wow of a meal. I use a 50/50 mix of lamb and beef mince because I believe it strikes the perfect balance between the richness of lamb and the fattiness of beef, but feel free to use whatever meat mince or plant-based meat substitute you like.

COOK THE MEAT: Heat a large frying pan over medium-high heat and add 1 tablespoon of olive oil. Break the meat into 2-inch pieces and, working in batches, add the pieces to the pan. Cook, undisturbed, until you achieve a good sear on the first side, then flip and sear one more side, about 4 minutes per side (no need to sear all sides). Remove from the pan and set aside while you sear the rest of the meat.

When all the meat is seared, drain any excess oil, and return all of the meat to the pan. Continue cooking over medium-high heat and begin breaking up the meat into smaller pieces. Stir in the harissa seasoning blend, ½ teaspoon kosher salt, harissa sauce, tomato paste, garlic, and 1 cup of water. Bring to a simmer, then reduce the heat to low. Continue simmering breaking up the meat until it's a very fine mince, about 15 minutes. If the pan starts to look dry, add more water.

MAKE THE FETA DRESSING: Crumble ¼ cup of the feta into a medium bowl. Add 2 tablespoons of the brine plus the yogurt, garlic, lemon zest, ¼ teaspoon salt, and a few cracks of pepper. Mix well and set aside.

MAKE THE CUCUMBER SALAD: In a medium bowl, toss together the cucumber, shallot, parsley, mint, lemon juice, and a pinch of salt. Toss to combine.

ASSEMBLE AND SERVE: Toast the pitas in a toaster or under a grill. Fill with the meat mixture, the cucumber salad, rocket, extra feta, and the feta dressing. Serve with more feta dressing for dipping and lemon wedges.

HOT TIP

Not all jarred harissas are created equal. Some come in the form of a sauce, as called for here, while some are more of a paste. If substituting with harissa paste in this recipe, skip the tomato paste and add an extra ½ cup of water or so to thin out the consistency. Harissas also vary in heat level so be sure to taste test all before using to avoid accidentally over spicing.

PORTERHOUSE WITH JAMMY TOMATOES

1 (2½- to 3-pound) porterhouse (T-bone) steak

1 pound campari tomatoes or any small sweet tomatoes, halved

Pinch of fennel pollen or crushed fennel seeds, plus more for serving

2 tablespoons hot honey

Extra-virgin olive oil

Kosher and flaky salt

Serves 2 to 4

This dish feels less like a steak and more like an event. It's inspired by the famous Tuscan bistecca alla Fiorentina, which is a supersized double-cut porterhouse—meaning it's 2 inches thick, and bone-in, which is as much for the flavour as it is for the drama. To get a perfectly cooked inside and caramelized outside, we're using the reverse sear method of starting the steak in the oven then finishing it on the barbecue.

PREP THE STEAK: Season your steak all over with 2 teaspoons of kosher salt, transfer it to a wire rack-lined roasting tray, and chill, uncovered, in the fridge overnight.

Remove the steak from the refrigerator, pat dry with a kitchen towel, and wipe away any juices that accumulated in the roasting tray. Let it sit at room temperature for at least 30 minutes before cooking.

Preheat the oven to 150°C.

ROAST THE TOMATOES AND THE STEAK: Line a roasting tray with foil and a wire rack, then brush the wire rack with olive oil. Arrange the tomatoes on the wire rack, cut side up. Season the tomatoes with a few pinches of salt, a few pinches of fennel pollen, and a drizzle of hot honey. Transfer to the oven and set a timer for 1 hour and 30 minutes.

Once the timer goes off, reduce the oven temperature to 140°C and add the steak onto the rack to roast along with the tomatoes. Cook until the tomatoes are shriveled and the steak reaches 45°C for medium-rare, 30 to 45 minutes. Remove both from the oven and set the tomatoes aside.

While the tomatoes and steak are roasting, preheat the grill to medium-high.

SEAR THE STEAK: Add the steak to the barbecue and sear until good char marks form, 3 to 5 minutes per side. Don't turn off the barbecue.

Transfer the steak to a cutting board and carve the meat off the bone. Throw the bone back on the grill for 3 to 5 minutes per side to caramelize any meat left behind. (Gnawing the meat off the bone at the end of the meal is my dad's favourite part.) Also, if at this point you realize the meat is underdone to your liking, place the steak back on the grill to cook for a few extra minutes until it reaches your desired doneness.

SERVE: Slice the steak into ½- to 1-inch-thick pieces. Arrange the slices on a platter along with the roasted bone and jammy tomatoes. Finish with a drizzle of olive oil, a sprinkle of flaky salt, and a pinch of fennel pollen.

BALSAMIC BRAISED SHORT RIBS

2 pounds boneless beef short ribs, or 3½ pounds bone-in short ribs

2 tablespoons plain flour

1 tablespoon vegetable oil, or more as needed

8 medium shallots, peeled and thinly sliced

6 garlic cloves, thinly sliced

¼ cup tomato paste

2 cups dry red wine, such as Chianti

4 cups beef stock

½ cup balsamic vinegar

2 tablespoons light brown sugar

10 sprigs fresh thyme, leaves stripped

1 tablespoon crushed red pepper flakes

Finely chopped fresh chives for serving

Kosher salt

Serves 6

HOT TIP
Dusting the short ribs in flour will thicken the sauce as they cook; however, feel free to skip this step if you're gluten free.

Here, we're taking the classic and ever-so-popular red wine-braised short rib formula and giving it a mini makeover with the addition of sweet brown sugar, tangy balsamic vinegar, and lots and lots of jammy shallots. Oh, then spooning it over mashed potatoes or polenta. What's not to love?

Preheat the oven to 150°C.

SEAR THE SHORT RIBS: Arrange the beef in a roasting tray, pat dry with a kitchen towel, and season with salt and a light dusting of flour, tapping off any excess.

Heat a large cast-iron casserole dish over medium-high heat, then add the vegetable oil. Working in batches, sear the beef until caramelized on all sides, about 3 minutes per side. Return the browned beef to the roasting tray and set aside.

SAUTÉ THE SHALLOTS: Drain any excess fat in the pan, leaving behind just enough oil to coat the bottom. Adjust the heat to medium-low and add the shallots and a pinch of salt. Use a wooden spoon to stir the shallots and scrape up any browned beef bits from the bottom of the pan. Cook, stirring occasionally, until the shallots begin to soften, 5 to 7 minutes.

Add the garlic and tomato paste and cook, stirring, until the tomato paste starts to caramelize and stick to the pot, 3 to 5 minutes.

Pour in the wine and use your spoon to scrape up more of the browned bits from the bottom of the pan. Cook until the wine has reduced by about two-thirds, 5 to 7 minutes. Add the stock, vinegar, and brown sugar and stir to combine.

BRAISE THE SHORT RIBS: Return the short ribs to the pot along with the thyme and pepper flakes. Bring to a boil, turn off the heat, cover tightly with a lid, and carefully transfer the braise to the oven.

Cook until the meat is fork tender, 2 to 3 hours for boneless short ribs or 3 to 4 hours for bone-in.

SERVE: Garnish with chives and serve. Pairs well with A Good Mash (page 127) and Pecorino Polenta (page 173).

bevs

DIRTY MARTINI WITH BLUE CHEESE-STUFFED OLIVES

For 1 Cocktail

2 ounces vodka or gin

1 ounce olive brine

½ ounce dry vermouth

Blue Cheese-Stuffed Olives (recipe follows), for serving

For 10 Cocktails

2½ cups vodka or gin

1¼ cups olive brine

⅔ cup dry vermouth

⅓ cup filtered water

Blue Cheese-Stuffed Olives (recipe follows), for serving

For the Dirty Ice

Pitted olives

Olive brine

As a teenager there were few things that I was willing to admit were "cool" about my mother, but her go-to drink order was one of them: "Extra-dirty Grey Goose martini with blue cheese-stuffed olives, dirty ice on the side." It was, and still is, the epitome of chic.

PREP THE GLASSES: Chill your martini glass(es) in the freezer for at least 10 minutes.

FOR 1 COCKTAIL: Fill a cocktail shaker halfway with ice. Add the vodka or gin, olive brine, and vermouth. Shake vigorously for 60 seconds. The cocktail shaker should be so cold it hurts your hands and the ice should be thoroughly crushed. Strain into the chilled martini glass and garnish with three blue cheese-stuffed olives.

Transfer the ice left behind in the shaker—referred to as "dirty ice"— to a rocks glass and serve with a spoon alongside the martini. Spoon some of the dirty ice into your martini to keep it perfectly chilled as you sip.

FOR BATCHED COCKTAILS: Combine the vodka or gin, olive brine, vermouth, and water and chill in the freezer for at least 24 hours prior to serving.

TO MAKE BATCHED "DIRTY ICE": Place 1 pitted olive in each well of an ice cube tray. Cover with 2 parts water and 1 part olive brine. Freeze until solid.

SERVE: Keep the batched beverage in the freezer or in an ice bucket and encourage guests to serve themselves. Pour into chilled martini glasses (about 3½ ounces per glass) and finish with a "dirty ice" cube. Garnish each drink with three stuffed olives.

BLUE CHEESE-STUFFED OLIVES

1 (1½-ounce) piece Danish blue cheese

1 (8-ounce) jar large pitted green olives

Vodka or gin, as needed

Hand crumble the blue cheese into a small bowl. Add a small splash of vodka, gin, or water. Use a fork to mash the cheese into a chunky paste. Transfer to a piping bag or a large plastic zip-top bag with one corner snipped off. Pipe the filling into each olive. The olives can be stored in an airtight container in the refrigerator for up to 3 days.

PICKLED PEPPER MARTINI

For 1 Cocktail

2 ounces vodka or gin

½ ounce cornichon or pickle brine

½ ounce pickled pepper brine (I like pepperoncini brine)

½ ounce dry vermouth

Pickled peppers, for garnish

Cornichons, for garnish

Cocktail onions, for garnish

For 10 Cocktails

2½ cups vodka or gin

⅔ cup cornichon or pickle brine

⅔ cup pickled pepper brine (I like pepperoncini brine)

⅔ cup dry vermouth

⅓ cup filtered water

Pickled peppers, for garnish

Cornichons, for garnish

Cocktail onions, for garnish

I love drinking pickle brine (Claussen's forever and always), and when I was introduced to pickle backs in college (shots of liquor followed by a shot of pickle brine), I knew I had to make it into a martini. While we're at it, I also threw in some pickled pepper brine from my dear pepperoncini peppers because the jar was next to the pickles in the fridge and I figured it couldn't hurt. Confirming it didn't. Think dirty martini but with an extra-briny twist.

PREP THE GLASSES: Chill your martini glass(es) in the freezer for at least 10 minutes.

FOR 1 COCKTAIL: Fill a shaker halfway with ice. Add the vodka or gin, cornichon brine, pepper brine, and vermouth. Shake vigorously for 60 seconds. The cocktail shaker should be so cold it hurts your hands and the ice should be thoroughly crushed.

SERVE: Strain into the chilled martini glass and garnish with pickled peppers, cornichons, and cocktail onions.

Transfer the shards left behind—referred to as the "dirty ice"—in the shaker to a short rocks glass and serve with a spoon alongside the martini. Spoon some of the dirty ice into your martini to keep it perfectly chilled as you sip.

FOR BATCHED COCKTAILS: Combine the vodka or gin, cornichon brine, pepper brine, vermouth, and water. Chill in the freezer for at least 24 hours prior to serving.

SERVE: Keep the batched beverage in the freezer or in an ice bucket and encourage guests to serve themselves. Pour into chilled martini glasses (about 3½ ounces per glass) and garnish with pickled peppers, cornichons, and cocktail onions.

LAMBRUSCO NEGRONI

For 1 Cocktail

1 ounce gin

1 ounce Campari

2 ounces Lambrusco, well chilled

Sweet vermouth, to taste (optional)

Orange slice, for serving

1 green olive, for serving

Extra-virgin olive oil, for serving (optional)

A classic Negroni doesn't always do it for me. Composed of gin, sweet vermouth, and Campari, it's bitter, a little too sweet, and, in my humble opinion, begging for some carbonation. Here I've swapped sweet vermouth for a slightly less sweet and far fizzier red wine: Lambrusco! Honestly, where has this sparkling red wine been all of my life?

Add a large ice cube to a rocks glass along with the gin and Campari and stir until chilled. Top with Lambrusco, sweet vermouth (if using), an orange slice, an olive, and a drizzle of olive oil if you're feeling crazy.

HOT TIP
I'm not one for rules, but one I strictly abide by is not batching carbonated cocktails. Anything with soda water or sparkling wine MUST be made to order.

SPICY SALTY RANCH WATER

For 1 Cocktail

1 (12-ounce) glass bottle Topo Chico, very well chilled

2 ounces blanco tequila, very well chilled

2 jalapeños, 1 thinly sliced and 1 frozen

1 lime, juiced (about 2 tablespoons)

Pinch of sea salt

Lime wedge

Tajin, for garnish (optional)

Shout-out to my Texas-born sister-in-law, and now Texas-resident older brother, for introducing me to ranch water. For those who are unfamiliar, ranch water may seem like just a tequila soda with lime juice, but it's so much more than that. The magic lies in the construction of the ranch water. By pouring tequila directly into a bottle of Topo Chico, it maintains maximum carbonation of the mineral water AND, since the bottle is fully enclosed, you won't catch a whiff of tequila while you sip, making for a more pleasant drinking experience. It's also kinda chic, no? This is that same OG method, but with a pinch of salt and a kick from sliced and grated jalapeño.

CHILL YOUR INGREDIENTS: A very, very crucial element to the success of ranch water is thoroughly chilling all the liquids since it's not getting poured over ice. Chill the Topo Chico in the fridge and the tequila in the freezer at least overnight, but the longer the better. Remember to throw a jalapeño in the freezer while you're at it.

ASSEMBLE: Use a Microplane to grate the frozen jalapeño onto a cutting board (see Hot Tip).

Take a few big sips of the Topo Chico to make room for the other ingredients. Add the tequila, lime juice, a pinch of salt, a few slices of jalapeño, and some of the grated jalapeño.

Use a lime wedge to wet the rim and the side of the bottle. Sprinkle with Tajin to the best of your ability. This is messy and extremely optional, but Tajin lovers like me will understand. Serve.

HOT TIP
Wear kitchen gloves while handling the grated and sliced jalapeño, wash your hands and under your fingernails throughly, and avoid touching your eyes afterward. As a girl who wears contact lenses, I am all too familiar with the pain of pepper in the eye.

PICANTE PIÑA

For 1 Cocktail

1 heaping cup frozen pineapple cubes

2 tablespoons unsweetened coconut cream

½ cup coconut water

1½ ounces Chilli-Infused Rum (recipe follows)

1 Fresno chilli, for garnish

For 4 Cocktails

4 heaping cups frozen pineapple cubes

½ cup unsweetened coconut cream

2 cups coconut water

6 ounces Chilli-Infused Rum (recipe follows)

4 Fresno chillies, for garnish

May I interest you in a spicy, frozen, blended piña colada that's made with no artificial or added sugars, all thanks to the natural sweetness of fresh (and then frozen) pineapple? Great, read on. While I adore the flavour of a sweetened coconut cream à la Coco López, it doesn't always agree with my stomach. So I wanted to create a version of my favourite frozen bev that I can consume sans tummy ache. The secret? We're relying on the natural sweetness of fresh then frozen pineapple and the natural creaminess of organic unsweetened coconut cream. The rum, however, is definitely not organic. Whole fresh pineapple has significantly more flavour and sweetness than store-bought frozen or pre-chopped pineapple.

BLEND THE PIÑA: In a blender, combine the frozen pineapple, coconut cream, coconut water, and chilli-infused rum. Blend until smooth. Garnish with a Fresno chilli and serve.

HOT TIP

To freeze whole pineapple, first purchase the pineapple a few days before you plan on making these so it has time to fully ripen. When you're ready to freeze it, remove the outer peel and discard. Core and dice the pineapple into 1- to 2-inch pieces. Arrange in a single layer on a roasting tray and chill in the freezer for 4 hours, then transfer the pineapple to a zip-top bag and freeze overnight.

CHILLI-INFUSED RUM

2 cups light rum

3 Fresno chillies, roughly chopped

Combine the rum and Fresno chillies in an airtight container, ideally glass. Let the mixture sit at room temperature for at least 12 hours or up to a week, giving the container a shake every now and then to speed up the infusion. Strain out the chillies before serving the rum.

CUCUMBER MELON SPRITZES

Makes Enough for 8 Cocktails

For the Cucumber Melon Puree

½ a ripe honeydew melon, seeded and roughly chopped

1 Persian cucumber, roughly chopped

1 cup coconut water, plus more as needed

Honey, to taste (optional)

For 1 Cocktail

Cucumber Melon Hugo Spritz

2 ounces Cucumber Melon Puree

½ ounce elderflower liqueur (I like St-Germain)

½ ounce freshly squeezed lime juice

4 ounces Prosecco, chilled

Soda water, chilled

3 honeydew melon balls, for garnish

1 sprig of mint, for garnish

For 1 Cocktail

Cucumber Melon Vodka Spritz

2 ounces Cucumber Melon Puree

1½ ounces vodka (I like Grey Goose Le Poire here)

½ ounce freshly squeezed lime juice

Soda water, chilled

3 honeydew melon balls

1 sprig of mint, for garnish

Every August and September, tennis fans from far and wide flock to Queens NY to attend the US Open tennis tournament. While some are passionate about the sport, others are more passionate about posting a picture of a Honey Deuce, the signature drink of the US Open, on their Instagram story. These drinks are inspired by the Honey Deuce but actually taste nothing like the infamous raspberry lemonade cocktail. Instead, I've embraced the light and refreshing flavours of honeydew and packaged it up in spritz form. A spritz so nice, she made it twice! No, your eyes do not deceive you, this recipe is a two in one, and that is because the two versions of this recipe that I tested were both so delicious, I couldn't bear the thought of excluding one.

MAKE THE PUREE: In a blender, combine the melon, cucumber, and 1 cup of coconut water and blend until smooth. Adjust the sweetness to your liking with your sweetener of choice (I like honey). The puree can be used immediately or transferred to an airtight container and stored in the fridge for up to 3 days.

FOR THE CUCUMBER MELON HUGO SPRITZ: In a large stemmed wineglass, combine the cucumber melon puree, elderflower liqueur, and lime juice and swirl to combine. Fill the glass three-quarters of the way with crushed ice and top off with chilled Prosecco. Finish with a splash of soda water. Garnish with melon and fresh mint.

FOR THE CUCUMBER MELON VODKA SPRITZ: In a large stemmed wineglass, combine the cucumber melon puree, vodka, and lime juice and swirl to combine. Fill the glass three-quarters of the way with crushed ice and top off with chilled soda water. Garnish with melon and fresh mint.

PASSION FRUIT MEZCALITA

For 1 Cocktail

Tajin, as needed

1 lime wedge

1 fresh passion fruit, halved (optional but encouraged)

1½ ounces mezcal (I like Madre)

1 ounce passion fruit liqueur (I like Chinola)

1 ounce freshly squeezed lime juice

Sea salt

For 10 Cocktails

2 cups mezcal

1¼ cups passion fruit liqueur (I like Chinola)

1¼ cups freshly squeezed lime juice

Sea salt

Lime wedges, as needed

10 fresh passion fruits, halved (optional but encouraged)

I find an excuse to make this cocktail any time I'm lucky enough to find fresh passion fruit at the grocery store. It's quite honestly the perfect fruit for a cocktail—sweet and slightly sour, which in this case really shines against the smoky backdrop of mezcal and spicy Tajin. Unfortunately, sourcing fresh passion fruit can be a challenge here in the North Eastern US. Luckily, a good passion fruit-flavoured liqueur (I love Chinola) is flavourful (and delicious) enough to convince me that the fresh passion fruit is technically optional here.

PREPARE YOUR GLASS(ES): Pour some Tajin onto a plate. Run a lime wedge around the rim of a rocks glass then press the rim into the Tajin to coat. Fill the glass to the top with crushed ice. Scoop out the centre of half of a fresh passion fruit into the glass. Reserve the other half for garnish.

FOR 1 COCKTAIL: Fill a cocktail shaker halfway with ice and add the mezcal, passion fruit liqueur, lime juice, and a pinch of sea salt. Shake vigorously for 60 seconds. The cocktail shaker should be so cold it hurts your hands. Strain the cocktail into the prepared glass. Nestle the remaining half of the passion fruit on top and serve.

FOR BATCHED COCKTAILS: Combine the mezcal, passion fruit liqueur, lime juice, and a few pinches of sea salt in a large jug. Mix to combine, cover, and store in the fridge for at least 3 hours or up to overnight. To serve, measure about 3½ ounces of the batched mix and pour into a prepared glass. Nestle half of the passion fruit on top and serve.

BOOZY BLUEBERRY BASIL LEMONADE

For 1 Cocktail

1½ ounces vodka or gin

1 ounce freshly squeezed lemon juice

1 teaspoon Blueberry Jam (page 250) or store-bought

5 fresh basil leaves, torn into ½ inch pieces

4 ounces soda water, chilled

For 10 Cocktails

2 cups vodka or gin (optional)

1¼ cups freshly squeezed lemon juice

¼ cup Blueberry Jam (page 250) or store-bought

5 cups filtered water or club soda

½ bunch fresh basil leaves, roughly torn

Lemon slices, for serving

One of the most quintessential Nantucket cocktails is blueberry vodka lemonade, all thanks to Cisco Brewers/Triple Eight Distillery's blueberry-flavoured vodka. Made with real berries, this vodka tastes like a shot of blueberry jam. Mix it with refreshingly tart lemonade on a hot summer night and that's paradise to me. This recipe is my way of recreating the beverage when I'm off island and Triple Eight is hard to come by. I'm subbing in unflavoured vodka and a literal shot of blueberry jam, and if you close your eyes it almost tastes like you're on island.

FOR 1 COCKTAIL: Fill a cocktail shaker halfway with ice and add the vodka or gin, lemon juice, blueberry jam, and torn basil leaves and shake vigorously.

SERVE: Dirty dump into a glass (meaning no straining, ice goes in too!), add more ice if desired, and top with 4 ounces of chilled soda water, or more to taste.

FOR BATCHED COCKTAILS: In a large container, whisk together the vodka or gin (if using), lemon juice, and blueberry jam. Store the lemonade concentrate in the refrigerator for up to 2 days until ready to serve.

If using water, in a large jug combine the lemonade concentrate and 5 cups of filtered water and stir to combine. To serve, fill glasses three-quarters full with crushed ice and pour over the lemonade. Top with a few pieces of torn basil leaves and a lemon slice.

If using soda water, do not premix it with the concentrate, as the carbonation will go flat. Instead, prepare each glass fresh. To serve, fill glasses three-quarters full with crushed ice. Pour in about 3⅓ ounces of the lemonade concentrate, then add about ½ cup of soda water. Top with a few pieces of torn basil leaves and a lemon slice.

JALAPEÑO MICHELADA

For 1 Cocktail

Tajín

2 lime wedges

1.5 ounces Tomatillo Salsa Verde (page 213)

Maggi Seasoning Sauce or Worcestershire sauce, for serving

Green hot sauce, such as El Yucateco Green Habanero Sauce, or Tabasco Green Pepper, for serving

1 (16-ounce) can Mexican beer, such as Modelo, well chilled

If you like Bloody Marys and you like beer, then boy, are you going to LOVE a michelada. It's a magical mash-up of the two: salty, savoury, and a little spicy. This particular version uses our homemade (duh) Tomatillo Salsa Verde in place of the typical red tomato-based michelada mixes that more closely resemble a typical Bloody Mary. Trust me, it's good.

RIM YOUR GLASS: Pour some Tajín onto a plate. Run a lime wedge around the rim of a tall glass, then press the rim into the Tajín to coat.

ASSEMBLE AND SERVE: Add the salsa verde to the glass along with a few dashes of Maggi and hot sauce to taste, then add ice. Pour in as much beer as you can fit and finish with a squeeze of lime. Serve the remaining beer on the side to top off as you sip.

GARDEN MERE-Y

Makes Enough for 10 Cocktails

For the Garden Mere-y Mix

2 pounds tomatoes, roughly chopped

2 mini cucumbers, roughly chopped

1 Cubanelle pepper, stemmed

2 tablespoons fresh lemon juice, plus more to taste

1 tablespoon chopped Calabrian chillies, or more for extra spicy

1 small shallot, peeled

1 small garlic clove, peeled

1 teaspoon grated fresh horseradish, or prepared horseradish

1 teaspoon kosher salt

For 1 Cocktail

2 ounces vodka

5 ounces Garden Mere-y Mix

Hot sauce, to taste
(I like Tabasco)

Pickle juice, to taste
(I like Claussen)

Mini kosher dill pickles, for garnish (I like Claussen)

Cherry tomato, for garnish

If you haven't realized by now, I LOVE tomatoes. Big tomatoes, small tomatoes, fresh tomatoes, canned tomatoes, you name it. Unshockingly, I also love Bloody Marys, but every time I come across a lacklustre cup of ketchup-y goo disguised as a Bloody, a small part of me dies inside. In a world filled with so many tomato opportunities, this is what we've settled for? Well I've chosen a different destiny, showing the Bloody Mary full respect by giving it the gazpacho treatment. If you're unfamiliar, gazpacho is a chilled soup consisting of a perfectly balanced blend of juicy tomatoes and vegetables, so good you'll want to drink it. With vodka. And thus the Garden Mere-y was born.

MAKE THE GARDEN MERE-Y MIX: In a blender, combine the tomatoes, cucumbers, Cubanelle pepper, lemon juice, Calabrian chillies, shallot, garlic, horseradish, and salt. Blend until smooth. Chill for at least 4 hours in the fridge before serving. The mix can be refrigerated in an airtight container for up to 3 days, or frozen for up to 6 months.

ASSEMBLE AND SERVE: For 1 cocktail, fill a tall glass three-quarters of the way with ice. Add the vodka, Garden Mere-y mix, a few dashes of hot sauce, and a splash of pickle juice. Stir until combined. Garnish with a mini dill pickle and cherry tomato. Serve.

baking

HEIRLOOM TOMATO GALETTE

For the Pastry

2 cups plain flour, plus more for dusting

1½ sticks (12 tablespoons) unsalted butter, well chilled and cut in tablespoon-size pieces

2 teaspoons kosher salt

⅓ cup ice water, plus more as needed

1 tablespoon apple cider vinegar

For the Filling

4 to 6 large heirloom tomatoes, preferably a mix of sizes and colours, sliced ¼ inch thick

5 cherry tomatoes, preferably a mix of colours, thinly sliced

¼ cup Basil Parsley Pesto (page 144), plus more for serving

1½ ounces freshly grated Parmesan or pecorino cheese (about ⅓ cup)

1 medium egg, beaten

8 ounces stracciatella or burrata cheese

¼ cup fresh basil leaves, for serving

1 lemon, zested

Kosher salt, flaky salt, and freshly ground black pepper

HOT TIP

You can use the same pastry dough for sweet and savoury pies! For sweet preparations, just sprinkle it with demerara sugar instead of Parm.

I formally introduce you to our cover star, and one of the first real recipes that I ever developed. This heirloom tomato galette has been with me since the beginning, and it's what gave me, and my parents, hope that I may actually have a future with this whole cooking thing. So let this be the motivation you need to follow your dreams, or to bake this recipe. Both honorable pursuits.

MAKE THE PASTRY: Combine the flour, butter, and salt in a food processor. Pulse until the butter is about the size of peas. Add the ice water and vinegar and continue to pulse until a shaggy dough forms, adding more ice water, a drizzle at a time, as needed.

Dust a flat work surface with flour. Transfer the dough to the surface and gently knead until no dry spots remain. Avoid overworking the dough. Form the dough into a round disk, then wrap in cling film and chill in the fridge for at least 2 hours, or preferably overnight.

Preheat the oven to 200°C and line a baking tray with parchment paper.

PREP YOUR TOMATOES: Salt the sliced heirloom and cherry tomatoes and arrange them in a single layer on a kitchen towel-lined baking tray. Allow the tomatoes to drain and release excess moisture for at least 10 minutes.

ROLL OUT THE DOUGH: Lightly dust the work surface with flour and, using a rolling pin, roll the dough into a large circle, about 15 inches in diameter. Carefully transfer the dough to the prepared baking tray.

BUILD YOUR GALETTE: Spread the pesto in the centre of the dough, leaving a 1- to 2-inch border at the edges. Sprinkle half of the Parmesan on top of the pesto and then layer the large tomatoes over the Parm. Top the large tomatoes with the small tomatoes.

Fold the crust up and over the edges of the tomatoes; it's perfectly okay that the edges are uneven. Lightly brush the exposed crust with the beaten egg and sprinkle it with the remaining Parmesan.

Bake until the crust is lightly browned, 45 to 55 minutes. Remove from the oven and allow the galette to cool on the baking tray for about 15 minutes and then carefully transfer it to a wire rack to cool to room temperature.

GARNISH AND SERVE: Top the tomato centre with stracciatella, extra pesto, basil leaves, lemon zest, flaky salt, and pepper. Slice and serve.

CATHEAD BISCUITS AND BLUEBERRY JAM

4 cups all-purpose or unbleached cake flour, plus more as needed

2 tablespoons baking powder

2 teaspoons fine sea salt

1 stick (8 tablespoons) unsalted butter, cold

2 cups buttermilk

Blueberry Jam, for serving (recipe follows)

Makes 10 large or 20 small biscuits

My family has always planned trips around food, and there were a few non-negotiables whenever visiting extended family in North Carolina: including cathead biscuits with country ham. What is a cathead biscuit you ask? Well, it's a biscuit about as big as a cat's head, y'all!!! No seriously. That's how they got their name (allegedly). These are not your typical flaky layered biscuits. They're almost like a drop biscuit, super tender and fluffy, like little biscuit clouds. While these biscuits would make a great country ham or breakfast sandwich vehicle, instead I've paired them with a homemade blueberry jam as a nod to my favourite restaurant from my college town in South Carolina, Tupelo Honey, which served free biscuits and blueberry jam in place of a bread basket (iconic).

Preheat the oven to 240°C. Line 2 large baking trays with silicone baking mats or parchment paper and set aside.

MAKE THE DOUGH: In a large bowl, stir together the flour, baking powder, and salt. Using the largest side of a box grater, grate the cold butter into the bowl, then use your hands to gently incorporate the butter into the flour, ensuring that each piece of butter is coated.

Pour in 1 cup of the buttermilk; use a fork to stir and mix. Add the remaining 1 cup of buttermilk and mix until just combined into a shaggy dough that is just beginning to hold together—try not to overwork the dough.

The dough will be sticky, so lightly coat your hands with flour before handling. Break off pieces of dough about the size of a tennis ball for large biscuits or a golf ball for small biscuits. Gently shape them into rounds without compacting the dough or smoothing the rough texture of the exterior. You want the dough to remain somewhat shaggy on the outside to maximize the surface area that'll crisp up in the oven.

BAKE THE BISCUITS: Place the biscuits on the prepared baking trays, leaving space in between them as the biscuits will almost double in size in the oven. You should have about 10 large or 20 small biscuits total.

Bake until the biscuits are golden, 15 to 20 minutes for large or 8 to 10 minutes for small. Serve warm with blueberry jam.

CONTINUED

CATHEAD BISCUITS AND BLUEBERRY JAM

CONTINUED

BLUEBERRY JAM

4 cups blueberries, thoroughly washed and dried, any leaves or stems removed

1 cup sugar

1 tablespoon fresh lemon juice

Makes 2 cups

The beauty of this homemade jam is that blueberries have a naturally high amount of fruit pectin, meaning you can make a super simple jam without any special equipment or ingredients or feeling like you need a degree in chemistry.

MAKE THE JAM: In a large saucepan, combine the blueberries, sugar, and lemon juice. The jam will bubble up quite a bit as it cooks so use a pan that's at least 2½ quarts so it doesn't boil over.

Place the pan over medium-high heat. Use a potato masher or wooden spoon to smash the berries and release their juices and bring to a boil. Allow the mixture to gently boil for 15 minutes, stirring and scraping the bottom and sides of the pan occasionally so it doesn't burn. Reduce the heat as needed to keep the mixture from boiling over.

To test if the jam has cooked long enough, place a teaspoon of the mixture on a small plate and place it in the freezer for about 5 minutes. When you remove it from the freezer, the consistency should resemble sticky jam, not runny loose syrup. Turn off the heat and let the mixture cool before using or storing.

STORE THE JAM: I am not a canning expert (yet), so I can't guide you go through the whole canning and preserving process (although you absolutely can). Instead, I recommend doing as I do and portioning your jam into 8-ounce deli containers or jars. Store one in your fridge for up to a week and the rest in the freezer for up to a year.

OLIVE OIL CAKE WITH PEACHES AND CREAM

For the Olive Oil Cake

¾ cup extra-virgin olive oil, plus more for preparing the pan

1½ cups plain flour, plus 1 tablespoon for dusting

1 teaspoon kosher salt

1 teaspoon baking powder

¼ teaspoon bicarbonate of soda

1 cup sugar, plus more for dusting and macerating

1 tablespoon freshly grated lemon zest

2 medium eggs, at room temperature

1 cup whole milk, at room temperature

1 tablespoon fresh lemon juice

2 pounds fruit of your choice, in this case peaches, sliced

Vanilla Bean Whipped Cream or Vanilla Buttercream (see below), for serving

Vanilla Bean Whipped Cream

2 cups cold double cream

⅓ cup icing sugar

2 teaspoons vanilla bean paste

Vanilla Bean Buttercream

1 batch of Marshmallow Meringue (page 256)

4 sticks (32 tablespoons) softened unsalted butter, cubed into tablespoon-size pieces

Serves 8

My mom, like myself, is notoriously not a baker, so on special occasions, she'd treat us to a store-bought angel food cake, a can of Reddi Wip, and a carton of strawberries. Then during my private chef days, I was introduced to the famous peaches and cream pie at Briermere Farms. This is basically a combination of those two desserts, using my all-time favourite olive oil cake recipe and whatever fruit is in season, although I'm partial to peaches. For the whipped topping I've included two options: a simple three-ingredient whipped cream and a slightly more complicated Italian buttercream. While the whipped cream is easy and delicious, the buttercream is much more stable in hot and humid temperatures. So if you're serving this on a hot summer day, or assembling it in advance, I highly suggest opting for the buttercream.

Preheat the oven to 190°C.

PREP THE CAKE PAN: Coat an 8-inch round cake pan with olive oil, line the bottom of the pan with parchment paper, and lightly brush the parchment with olive oil. Coat the inside of the pan with 1 tablespoon of flour, turning the pan over and tapping out any excess.

COMBINE THE DRY INGREDIENTS: In a large bowl, whisk together the remaining 1½ cups of flour, the salt, baking powder, and bicarbonate of soda.

MIX THE BATTER: In the bowl of a stand mixer fitted with the paddle attachment, or in a large bowl if you plan to use a hand mixer, combine 1 cup of the sugar and the lemon zest. Use your fingers to massage the lemon zest into the sugar to bring out the oils in the lemon zest. Add the eggs and beat on high speed until light and fluffy, 3 to 5 minutes. Switch the speed to medium and slowly stream in the olive oil. Beat until fully incorporated, about 2 minutes. Add the milk and lemon juice and beat on low until just combined.

COMBINE WET AND DRY: Stop the mixer and add half of the dry ingredients to the wet, and beat on low speed until most of the flour is incorporated. Stop the mixer, and add the remaining dry ingredients. Beat on low until just combined. Do not overmix or your cake will be tough.

CONTINUED

OLIVE OIL CAKE WITH PEACHES AND CREAM

CONTINUED

BAKE THE CAKE: Pour the batter into the prepared pan and sprinkle 2 tablespoons of sugar evenly over the top. Bake until a toothpick inserted into the centre comes out mostly clean, 35 to 40 minutes.

COOL THE CAKE: Allow the cake to cool in the pan for about 10 minutes. Carefully run a paring knife around the edge of the cake to loosen it from the sides, remove the cake from the pan, and transfer to a wire rack to cool. Allow the cake to cool for at least 1 hour before slicing or serving.

MACERATE THE FRUIT: In a large bowl, combine the fruit with a few tablespoons of sugar, more or less depending on your preference and the natural sweetness of the fruit. Toss to coat and let sit for 10 to 15 minutes before serving.

PREPARE THE WHIPPED TOPPING: You can make either the whipped cream or the buttercream.

For the whipped cream, in the bowl of a stand mixer fitted with the whisk attachment or in a large bowl if you'd rather use a hand mixer, combine the cream, icing sugar, and vanilla bean paste. Whip on high speed until stiff peaks form, 2 to 3 minutes. Transfer to the fridge until you're ready to use. This will stay good and fluffy in the fridge for a few hours.

For the buttercream, prepare a batch of the marshmallow meringue according to the directions on page 256. Keep the mixer running on low speed and add in the butter 1 tablespoon at a time. Continue beating until the butter is fully incorporated and you achieve a smooth and silky consistency.

TO SERVE: If using the buttercream, spread it over the top of the cake and pile it high with fruit. This can be assembled and kept in the fridge or at room temperature a few hours in advance.

If using the whipped cream, slice the cake into eight equal pieces. Transfer to dessert plates and top each slice with a dollop of whipped cream and a serving of fruit. Serve right away.

DECONSTRUCTED PIE SUNDAES

For the Shortbread Crumble

1½ cups plain flour

¾ cup granulated sugar

⅓ cup packed light brown sugar

¼ teaspoon kosher salt

1½ sticks (12 tablespoons) unsalted butter, well chilled, cut in tablespoon-size pieces

For Apple "Pie" Sundae

5 medium crisp, tart apples, such as Honeycrisp or Granny Smith, peeled, cored, and cut into ½-inch dice (about 5 cups)

1 cup packed light brown sugar

2 tablespoons fresh lemon juice

1 tablespoon pumpkin pie spice

½ teaspoon vanilla bean paste

¼ teaspoon kosher salt

2 tablespoons cornflour

Vanilla ice cream, for serving

For Summer Fruit "Pie" Sundae

3 to 5 ripe stone fruits, such as peaches, plums, or nectarines, pitted and sliced (about 3 cups)

2 cups berries, such as blueberries, raspberries, blackberries, or hulled and sliced strawberries

1 cup packed light brown sugar

2 tablespoons fresh lemon juice

½ teaspoon vanilla bean paste

¼ teaspoon kosher salt

2 tablespoons cornflour

Vanilla ice cream, for serving

Serves 6 to 8

This recipe was born out of my need to micromanage pie the way Meg Ryan does in When Harry Met Sally *("I'd like the pie heated, and I don't want the ice cream on top; I want it on the side. And I'd like strawberry instead of vanilla, if you have it. If not, then no ice cream, just whipped cream, but only if it's real. If it's out of a can, then nothing.") Because even though pie has convinced everyone that it's low-maintenance, it is nothing short of toxic. It wants to be sliced but quickly becomes an oozy mess. It wants to be easy-breezy, but you can never know when the filling is fully cooked or the crust is going to be soggy. It wants to be the centrepiece at low-key summer dinners, but there's always too much left over. So I'm holding my boundaries and the madness stops here. Instead, we're batching out cooked summer or autumn fruit and a crust-like crumble, which you can serve any way you like, any time you like, ALWAYS with ice cream.*

Preheat the oven to 180°C.

MAKE THE CRUMBLE: In a large bowl, combine the flour, granulated sugar, brown sugar, and salt. Add the butter and use your hands to work the mixture until it resembles coarse crumbs. Press the mixture in your hands to form 1- to 2-inch clumps and transfer to a roasting tray. Bake until golden brown, 25 to 30 minutes. Remove from the oven and let cool.

Once cooled, break up any larger pieces and transfer the crumble to an airtight container.

COOK THE FRUIT: In a large saucepan, combine the fruits of choice, the brown sugar, lemon juice, any spices or flavourings, and salt. Bring to a simmer over medium-low heat and cook, stirring occasionally, until the fruit is soft but not completely mushy, 10 to 15 minutes.

While the fruit simmers, in a small bowl, whisk the cornflour with 2 tablespoons of water. Whisk the mixture into the softened fruit and simmer until the mixture thickens slightly, about 2 minutes more. Turn off the heat.

ASSEMBLE THE SUNDAES: Add a few scoops of vanilla ice cream to a bowl and top with the cooked fruit and shortbread crumble.

TO STORE: Once cooled, transfer both the crumble and the fruit into separate airtight containers. They'll keep in the fridge for up to 1 week or in the freezer for up to 6 months. Reheat the fruit before serving.

S'MORES ICE CREAM PIE

For the Graham Crust

12 whole honey graham crackers (about 1½ cups finely ground crumbs) or plain digestive biscuits

¼ cup sugar

¼ teaspoon kosher salt

¾ stick (6 tablespoons) unsalted butter, melted

For the Fudge

1 cup double cream

⅔ cup sugar

½ teaspoon vanilla extract

½ teaspoon sea salt

4 ounces semisweet chocolate, chopped

1 tablespoon unsalted butter

For the Ice Cream Filling

1 pint vanilla ice cream, softened

1 pint chocolate ice cream, softened

For the "Marshmallow" Meringue

4 medium egg whites

¼ teaspoon kosher salt

¼ teaspoon cream of tartar

1½ cups sugar

1 vanilla pod, seeds removed and reserved, or 2 teaspoons vanilla bean paste

Serves 8

When it comes to the debate of chocolate or vanilla, I'm team vanilla every time. Now before you come for me: I don't hate chocolate, but I do hate most chocolate-forward desserts. I find chocolate can be very overwhelming on the palate, therefore I prefer it as a secondary flavour. Which is why I love s'mores. They strike the perfect ratio of nutty graham cracker, sweet marshmallow, and bitter chocolate. Dessert synergy, if you will. This s'mores ice cream pie is the ultimate dessert synergy. Inspired by my favourite Hula Pie from The Juice Bar in Nantucket, it has a honey graham crust, a layer of rich fudge, and your fave ice cream flavour as a filling. I've added a mountain of toasted marshmallow meringue, which makes this pie a total showstopper.

MAKE THE CRUST: In a food processor, pulse the graham crackers or digestive biscuits until finely ground. Add the sugar, salt, and melted butter, then pulse until fully combined.

Transfer the crumb mixture to a 9-inch spring form pan, or an extra deep 9-inch tart pan with a removable bottom. Use the flat bottom of a measuring cup to firmly press the crumb mixture into the base of the pan and against the sides to form an even crust. Transfer into the freezer to set for at least an hour.

MAKE THE FUDGE: In a small saucepan, combine the cream, sugar, vanilla, and salt. Bring the mixture to a gentle simmer over medium-low heat. Whisk in the chocolate and turn off the heat. Continue whisking until the chocolate has melted and no lumps remain. Turn the heat back on to low, add the butter, and whisk until the sauce is shiny, another 30 seconds. Remove the pan from heat and transfer the sauce to a heatproof container. Set aside to cool.

Remove the crust from the freezer and spread an even ¼-inch-thick layer of fudge over the base of the crust, reserving leftover fudge for serving. Transfer back into the freezer to set for another hour.

CONTINUED

S'MORES ICE CREAM PIE

CONTINUED

FILL THE PIE WITH ICE CREAM: Scoop the softened ice cream into the crust, alternating scoops of vanilla and chocolate, then swirl them together with a rubber spatula. Use the spatula to smooth the top of the filling, pressing down to remove any air pockets.

Cover and transfer the pie to the freezer to set overnight.

MAKE THE MERINGUE: In the bowl of a stand mixer fitted with the whisk attachment, combine the egg whites, salt, and cream of tartar. Whip until foamy, then pause the mixer until the sugar is ready.

In a medium saucepan, combine the sugar and ⅓ cup of water. Bring to a gentle boil, stirring constantly, until the sugar syrup reaches 120°C.

Right before the sugar is done cooking, restart the mixer and beat the eggs on high. Carefully stream the sugar syrup into the mixer, pouring along the side of the bowl. Once all of the sugar has been added, continue whipping until you achieve medium to soft peaks, 5 to 7 minutes. Add the seeds from the vanilla pod once you've achieved your desired consistency. Turn off the mixer and use a blowtorch to toast the meringue in the bowl. Mix and repeat about 3 times. This will incorporate the toasted marshmallow flavour throughout. If you don't have a blowtorch, you can skip this step.

Meringue can be used right away or stored in an airtight container in the fridge for 2 to 3 days.

ASSEMBLE AND TORCH: Remove the pie from the freezer and carefully pop the frozen pie out of the cake or tart pan. Use a rubber spatula to dollop the meringue on top. Use a blowtorch to toast the outside of the meringue.

SERVE: To slice the pie, run a large, sharp knife under hot running water and wipe dry before each cut. This will help the knife glide through the pie, for clean slices. Reheat any remaining fudge sauce and serve on the side.

HOT TIP
If making meringue is too involved for you (I hear you I see you) you can easily substitute with store-bought marshmallow crème for a similar effect.

STICKY TOFFEE PUDDING

For the Cakes

½ stick plus 1 tablespoon (5 tablespoons) unsalted butter, softened, plus cold butter for greasing

10 pitted Medjool dates

1 cup plain flour

1¼ teaspoons baking powder

½ teaspoon bicarbonate of soda

¼ teaspoon sea salt

1 cup packed dark brown sugar

1 medium egg plus 1 medium egg yolk

1 teaspoon vanilla extract

Flaky salt, for serving

Vanilla ice cream, for serving

For the Toffee Sauce

2 cups packed light brown sugar

1 cup double cream

2 teaspoons sea salt

6 tablespoons unsalted butter

Makes 9 puddings

For the Americans in the room who aren't as familiar with this British-born dessert: It's not pudding like a Snack Pack pudding cup. It's a cake soaked in toffee sauce, and the cake is impossibly moist due to the incorporation of dates, which also impart a rich caramel flavour. My family always serves this with Christmas dinner, and I look forward to it all year long.

Preheat the oven to 180°C. Use the cold butter to grease the inside of nine 3.5-ounce ramekins.

PREP THE DATES: In a medium saucepan, combine the dates with 1 cup of water. Bring the mixture to a simmer over medium heat. As the dates cook, use a wooden spoon to break them up into a paste, leaving no large chunks. Cook until all of the water has been absorbed, 10 to 15 minutes. Transfer the mixture to a bowl and set aside to cool. No need to clean out the pan, we will reuse it for the toffee sauce.

MAKE THE CAKE BATTER: In a large bowl, whisk together the flour, baking powder, bicarbonate of soda, and salt.

In the bowl of a stand mixer fitted with the paddle attachment or in a large bowl if you plan to use a hand mixer, combine the 5 tablespoons of butter and the brown sugar. Beat on high speed until the mixture is light and fluffy, about 5 minutes. Add the egg, egg yolk, and vanilla and mix until well combined. Add the date mixture and mix until just combined. Stop the mixer and add the dry ingredients. Mix on low speed just until the flour disappears. Don't overmix.

BAKE THE CAKES: Evenly distribute the batter among the ramekins. Wipe the edges of the ramekins with a dampened kitchen towel so any drips won't burn. Arrange the ramekins in a baking tray and bake until a toothpick inserted into the middle of the cakes comes out mostly clean, 15 to 20 minutes. Transfer to a wire rack to cool for 10 to 15 minutes.

MAKE THE TOFFEE SAUCE: In the same small saucepan used to cook the dates, combine the brown sugar, cream, and salt. Bring to a low boil over medium heat and stir in the butter. Simmer until the sauce is slightly thickened, about 2 minutes, then turn off the heat.

CONTINUED

STICKY TOFFEE PUDDING

CONTINUED

SOAK THE CAKES: When the cakes have cooled slightly, carefully turn them out from the ramekins onto a cutting board. Use a serrated knife to slice off the raised rounded tops. Discard the scraps (or snack on them; they're delish).

Add 2 tablespoons of warm toffee sauce to the bottom of each ramekin, then return the cakes, placing them cut side up. Pour more toffee sauce on top of each cake, enough to coat, reserving extra toffee sauce for serving. Let the cakes sit and soak up the sauce for at least 30 minutes, or preferably overnight in the fridge.

Move the top oven rack to the upper third of the oven and preheat the grill.

Just before serving, reheat the reserved toffee sauce on the stove and grill the cakes until they are warmed through and the toffee sauce is bubbling, about 2 minutes. To reheat the cakes from refrigerated, transfer to a preheated 180°C degree oven until heated through, 10 to 15 minutes, then grill as above.

TO SERVE: Carefully unmold the cakes and plate them cut side down. Drizzle with more toffee sauce and sprinkle with flaky salt. Serve with vanilla ice cream.

HOT TIP
If you don't have ramekins, a muffin pan can be used in a pinch.

Making a Menu

One of the more challenging components of cooking for a large group, whether you're a private chef, a host/hostess, or a home cook, is constantly creating new menus that work with you, not against you. There are countless variables to consider, and it can be downright daunting. Throughout my years of experience, I've gathered some simple strategies to help make this process a little easier.

With most of my menus, my standard formula is a drink, a snack, a veg, a starch, a main, and dessert. Then, when determining what to make for each of those dishes, some things you need to consider are **budget, bandwidth, and flow.**

Let's start with the **budget**. First, decide how much you can spend, then work backward from there. A great way to keep costs down when creating a menu is to choose dishes that incorporate ingredients you already have and ingredients that are local to your area. It's much more affordable to throw a seafood feast when you're in a New England beach town than if you are somewhere hours away from the coastline.

Another way to cut down on grocery cost is to select dishes that use similar ingredients. A simple and straightforward way to achieve this is to stick to one type of cuisine (French, Thai, Vietnamese, Mexican, Italian) because dishes from the same region will inherently use similar ingredients. Not only does this cut down on grocery costs, but it will also cut down on waste.

As for **bandwidth**, you need to think about your **personal capacity**, as well as the **capacity of your work space** to execute this menu. When considering your personal capacity, I want you to be brutally honest with yourself, especially if you're a first-time host. Are you someone who can multitask in the kitchen and have four dishes firing at the same time? Or does that sound like your own personal hell? To avoid a mid-party meltdown, choose dishes that you've made before at a volume you are experienced with. This is not the time to experiment (respectfully). But also be kind and patient with yourself; you need to learn how to walk before you can run.

As a host, you need to prioritize being present with your guests rather than over-extending yourself with a complicated menu. A good dinner party is arguably 50 percent ambiance and 50 percent food and drink. In fact, some of my most fun dinner parties have been over a bucket of delivery fried chicken and batched martinis. Reason being, I was having fun, therefore my guests were having fun. With that said, do not hold yourself to private-chef-level expectations. When I am cooking dinner for a client, my menus are always more complex than if I were cooking for friends because it's my job and I'm not the one who's entertaining guests!

Remember, you are inviting people into your home and it's your job not just to feed them, but to make them feel welcomed and comfortable. Whenever you're hosting, think of your home as a restaurant and your role is with the front of house staff, not hiding in the kitchen as a line cook.

For example, I try to keep my guests oblivious to any and all stress; I strive to manage their expectations, and, when all else fails, I keep refilling their wineglasses until everyone is too wine happy to notice that I've overcooked the chicken. Think about a dining experience you've had where the food was objectively great but was overshadowed by the horrible service. Compared to a dining experience where the staff took such great care of you, you almost forget they got your order wrong three times.

Never forget that your guests are there to spend time with you! So you want to avoid retreating to the kitchen for large chunks of time if you can. However, if you're set on a menu that requires lots of attention in the kitchen, bring the party to you. Set up appetizers and drinks in the kitchen so that you can chat with everyone as you work. Or the reverse: cook everything ahead of time and simply reheat before serving. This is my preferred method.

When thinking about the **capacity of your workspace,** consider your counter space, fridge space, oven space, and available equipment. I used to live in an apartment where the kitchen was just a fridge, sink, stove, and 18 inches of counter space along the wall of my living room. I could literally be sitting on the end of the living room couch while stirring whatever was on the stove. Safe to say, this was not the place to bust out a three-course meal. However, it was ideal for a cosy couch dinner party, with one big pot of cosy slop (soup, chilli, stew, pasta) and some bowls and spoons. Bonus points for pre-slop snacks. Having people over for dinner doesn't have to mean making fancy food. Sometimes a home-cooked bowl of soup and curling up on the couch with your friends is all you need. Now swallow your ego and serve some slop!

A menu with good flow will feel like a synchronized swimming routine. Each dish independently vibing, not getting in each other's way, seamlessly dancing from cutting board to oven to serving platter. Flow is heavily reliant on proper bandwidth assessment. With that said, I like to choose dishes that use a variety of cooking methods so as not to create a bottleneck. For example: a room-temperature salad that requires no cooking, a side dish that cooks on the stove, a main dish that roasts in the oven, and a dessert that I can make ahead of time. And if you've really got the flow down you can time it so everything finishes cooking at the same time.

To do so, you need to map out how long each dish takes to cook and work backward from there. And when all else fails, a 90°C oven is a lifesaver when it comes to keeping food warm. Or you can take it a step further and do the restaurant/catering trick where you heat up plates or serving platters in warming drawers (a 90°C oven will also work) and the residual heat keeps food warm as it makes its way to your table.

Sample menus: Even though creating menus is one of the more challenging parts of my job as a private chef, it's also sometimes the most fun! So I've taken the recipes from this book and compiled them into seven dinner party menus for your enjoyment. Do I advise you, the reader, to re-create these menus all by yourself all in one day? Absolutely not! What are you, nuts? What I do advise is that you take these menus and tips as tokens of inspiration and guidance as you continue to explore the wonderful world of hosting!

Winter Holiday

Dirty Martini with Blue Cheese-Stuffed Olives
(PAGE 223)

Crispy Caviar Potatoes
(PAGE 51)

Lobster Bisque
(PAGE 83)

Radicchio with Hazelnuts and Brown Butter Vin
(PAGE 77)

Balsamic Braised Short Ribs
(PAGE 219)

Brown Buttered Broccoli
(PAGE 115)

A Good Mash
(PAGE 127)

Sticky Toffee Pudding
(PAGE 259)

Serves 6 to 8 people

Like a plaid wool blazer, there are some things that make the most sense during the months of November and December: vodka martinis, caviar, and braised short ribs. My family has an ongoing tradition of lobster bisque and sticky toffee pudding for Christmas dinner every year, and I'd like to pass the torch on to anyone willing and able.

The Prep: Three days before the party, I would do my first round of grocery shopping where I buy all of the pantry items that I need and only the refrigerated items for the recipes that I'm prepping in advance (as a NYC apartment dweller with a small fridge, not over-buying early in the week is key—keep this in mind for all menus!). Two days before the party I'd make: the brown butter vin, the pre-batched martinis (plus "dirty ice" and blue cheese-stuffed olives), sticky toffee pudding, and prep the caviar potatoes (boil, halve, and scoop). The day before the party, I'd do another round of grocery shopping (I always save seafood and lettuce greens for the last possible day). I'd then make the lobster bisque, the mashed potatoes, and the braised short ribs (these taste even better the next day). Then all that's left to do on the day of the party is make the broccoli, reheat the rest of the menu, assemble, and actually enjoy yourself. Happy holidays!!!

Hot Tip: The key to effortless entertaining is stretching out your responsibilities over the course of a few days or weeks. For a menu and occasion like this, I'd set the table a week in advance, or if you don't have a separate dining table, simply gather all of your table and serveware to confirm your inventory. I've been burned by saving this for the night before far too many times to find out that I'm short two serving platters, three napkins are missing, or I never replaced those wineglasses that we shattered during our last dinner party. One of my favourite tips is to use masking tape to label all of your serving platters with which dish you plan to serve them on, this way on the day of you don't even have to think about it and you can enlist the help of your guests to transfer dishes to their serving vessels.

Birthday

Pickled Pepper Martini
(PAGE 224)

Oysters with Classic Mignonette
(PAGE 47)

Crab Fried Rice
(PAGE 161)

Cabbage and Herb Salad
(PAGE 69)

Wok Lobster
(PAGE 155)

Duck Lettuce Wraps
(PAGE 207)

Cake
(store-bought is fine, cake on page 25 is by From Lucie)

Serves 6 to 8 people

This luxe and over-the-top fantasy menu is exactly what I, a Capricorn, aspire to have on my birthday table. It's sort of a fever dream Frankenstein of all of my favourite dishes from all of my favourite restaurants, brought together for one night only!

The Prep: For this menu, three days in advance of the party, I would do some grocery shopping, chop all of the garlic and ginger I need for all dishes, batch the martinis, prep the mignonette, make the sauces for the fried rice, cabbage salad and lettuce wraps (it's the same sauce!), and wok lobster, and cure the duck legs. Two days in advance I would confit the duck legs and finish prepping the cabbage and herb salad. One day before the party, I would finish grocery shopping, cook and breakdown the lobsters, cook the rice and spread it out in a roasting tray to let it dry out overnight, and finish prepping any veg that still needs to be done (herbs and veg for the fried rice, lobster noodles, and duck wraps). Then on the day of the party, all that's left to do is to pick up the cake and the oysters, fry the rice, cook the lobster noodles, finish the duck, assemble everything, and enjoy.

Hot Tip: A menu like this requires a lot of chopping and a lot of the same ingredients. To get through your food prep as fast as possible, instead of going recipe by recipe, go ingredient by ingredient. So on your prep day, chop all of the garlic you'll need for the entire menu, all of the ginger, all of the spring onions, and so on. This will save you so much time, energy, and cleanup. Something else that will save you time and energy? Outsourcing dessert. Yes, store-bought is more than fine; it's actually encouraged here.

Taco Party

Passion Fruit Mezcalita
(PAGE 235)

Spicy Salty Ranch Water
(PAGE 228)

Really Good Guac
(double recipe)
(PAGE 36)

Tomatoes and Corn
(double recipe)
(PAGE 116)

Herby Rice and Radish Salad
(PAGE 170)

Fish Tacos
(double recipe)
(PAGE 189)

Pork Tacos with Roasted Peach Salsa
(PAGE 210)

Serves 10 to 12 people

Because a good taco party calls for twice the tequila and twice the tacos. While taco parties should be observed year round, this menu is encouraged to be prepared during the summer months when produce is at its peak.

The Prep: Some of the dishes in this menu are impossible to prepare in advance, making the prep for this a little tricky, so I recommend recruiting the help of friends and family or opting for a potluck situation. However, if I were to execute this on my own, here is how I would do it: Four to five days ahead of the party, I would secure the avocados and peaches so that they're perfectly ripe for the party. Three days ahead of the party I would do the rest of the grocery shopping. Two days ahead of the party I would roast the pork shoulder, make the salsa verde, make the peach salsa, and pickle the shallots. One day before the party, I would squeeze a bunch of fresh lime juice and batch the passion fruit mezcalitas, make the herb puree and chop the veg for the rice salad, dice onion and coriander for the pork tacos, make the guac, and shave the cabbage and make the sauce for the fish tacos. The rest of the prep and cooking—and the purchasing of the fish—would likely need to be done the day of for optimal freshness.

Hot Tip: Sometimes when setting up a buffet station with things like tacos, you need to make the executive decision whether or not to pre-assemble each taco, or encourage guests to build their own. Now I go fifty-fifty on this, and ultimately it comes down to the number of guests I'm serving and the faith I have in my guests to execute the assembly correctly. If I suspect my guests may botch their tacos and put the fish taco toppings on their pork tacos (even after I've demonstrated it five thousand times and put up signage . . . we all know those people), then I will be assembling each individual taco. If I'm serving twenty-plus people and that's not an option, I'll set up two separate tables, one for each taco station with their respective toppings, to avoid any confusion. And no, I've never been relaxed ever!

Summer Clambake

Blueberry Basil Lemonade, Boozy or Not
(PAGE 236)

Hot Crab Dip
(PAGE 39)

Oysters Parm
(PAGE 31)

Heirloom Crab Cocktail
(PAGE 28)

Blueberry BBQ Grilled Chicken Salad
(PAGE 66)

Nantucket Clambake
(PAGE 176)

Deconstructed Pie Sundaes
(PAGE 255)

Serves 6 to 8 people

While you may know me as the private chef in the Hamptons, I'm a Nantucket girl at heart. I've spent summers there since I was only eighteen months old, and it has become a core part of my personal and culinary identity. This menu is my ode to Nantucket, where blueberries are sweet as can be, the shellfish is world class, and dinner is best served with a side of melted butter.

The Prep: With any seafood-forward menu, much of it cannot be cooked ahead of time. However, we can definitely get a good head start for ourselves. A clambake requires some specialty utensils, so at least a week prior I would track down my lobster crackers and enamelware and make sure I have enough for all of my guests. Three days before, I would make a big batch of blueberry jam, the blueberry BBQ sauce, blueberry vinaigrette, and blueberry lemonade mix. Two days before, I'd prepare the deconstructed pie sundaes, the tomato butter sauce and panko for the oysters, the gazpacho for the crab cocktail, and any dipping sauce to serve with the clambake. The day before, I would prepare the crab dip and clean out my fridge (to make room for the incoming lobsters). The morning of the party would be dedicated to sourcing and processing (cleaning/shucking) all of the seafood (a job you can hopefully pass off to an eager friend or family member). Plus, assembling and cooking the rest of the menu.

Hot Tip: My Nantucket clambake recipe was specifically developed to be made in a standard 8-quart stockpot (to serve 6 people), so that it would be accessible to as many home cooks as possible. However, if you thoroughly enjoy hosting, I highly recommend investing in large-scale cookware and serveware, like a 16-quart stockpot, extra-extra-large mixing bowls, and serving platters. These may feel like an unnecessary upgrade, but trust me when I say they will just make your life significantly easier (if you can afford the storage space, that is).

Country Club

Jalapeño Michelada
(PAGE 241)

Garden Mere-y
(PAGE 242)

Lobster Avocado Salad
(PAGE 60)

Chive Crab Cakes
(PAGE 183)

Chicken Cutlet Club
(PAGE 97)

Hot Buttered Lobster Rolls
(PAGE 94)

Heirloom Tomato Galette
(PAGE 246)

Serves 8 to 10 people

A guilty pleasure of mine is Waspy country club culture. It's so camp. Adults wearing matching white outfits, playing sports, eating chicken salad, and drinking vodka at noon? Incredible. This menu is inspired by your typical country club food offering but with some New England flare. Perfect for ladies who lunch, or like day drinking over a nice meal (not brunch).

The Prep: If I were making this menu (and making it mini) I would start sourcing two to three weeks in advance. For catering supplies, I'd check restaurant supply stores and Amazon. For something like mini split-top buns, I'd check my local grocery stores to see if anyone carries them. If not, I'd look into ordering some or reluctantly making them from scratch. Executing this menu solo is ambitious to say the least, even for a trained professional like myself. But here is how I would attack it: Three days before the party, I would make the pesto and the pastry dough. Two days before the party I would make the purees for the michelada and the Garden Mere-y, herb salad dressing, and ranch dressing. The day before the party I would cook and break down the lobsters, shave the cabbage and cook the bacon for the club sandwiches, assemble the crab cakes, bake the biscuits, and make the jam. The day of the party, I would bake the tomato galette first thing in the morning and fry the cutlets and the crab cakes before guests arrived, then reheat them in the oven before serving. That way I'm not standing over the stove the entire party.

Hot Tip: Looking at this menu with my private chef hat on, my brain immediately tells me to make it mini. Mini biscuits, mini club sandwiches, mini lobster rolls, mini crab cakes, mini tomato galettes. This way, people get to try a little bit of everything! Whenever I do a mini menu like this, it's all about the details. Mini jam jars for the biscuits, cute toothpicks for the club sandwiches, mini split-top buns for the lobster rolls, and any fun accessories that make it feel professionally catered. You'd be surprised at how long these kinds of things can take to track down, so be sure to give yourself ample time.

Pasta Party

Lambrusco Negroni
(PAGE 227)

Ricotta with Fried Garlic
(PAGE 40)

Italian Chopped with Buffalo Mozzarella
(PAGE 56)

Roasted Broccoli with Caper Butter
(PAGE 120)

Broccoli Cavatelli
(PAGE 143)

Pink Lemon Pasta
(PAGE 151)

Bucatini and Meatballs
(PAGE 131)

Olive Oil Cake with Peaches and Cream
(PAGE 251)

Serves 8 to 10 people

Growing up in New Jersey meant that every party was a pasta party. No, seriously you could not go to a social function without finding a tray of ziti laying around somewhere. Honestly, I love that for us. This menu is inspired by those trays of ziti and the red sauce Italian American restaurants that feel like home.

The Prep: For this menu, two days ahead of the party I would make the red sauce and meatballs, the basil parsley pesto, the olive oil cake, and fry the garlic for the ricotta. The day before the party, I would grate a ton of Parmesan cheese, cube up a bunch of butter for the pastas, and prep the salad dressing and the rest of the salad and store all the ingredients in separate containers. Firing three pastas at one time in any home kitchen is going to be an uphill battle. Instead, I advise you to cook the bucatini and cavatelli first, undercooking them by a few minutes, transferring the cooked pasta into pots with their respective sauces, and holding off on simmering the pasta in the sauce until right before serving. The lemon pasta will benefit the most from being prepared à la minute. Also, reuse the pasta water for all pasta cooking (you can use a kitchen spider or slotted spoon to take the cooked pasta out of the water when it's done), so you're not waiting forever for water to boil.

Hot Tip: A carb-heavy menu, or in this case a pasta-heavy menu, is my favourite way to host on a budget. It stretches expensive proteins, it reheats well, and it's always a crowd pleaser. What can I say, people love pasta. In my experience, I find that people are much more likely to treat themselves to their favourite foods when they're at a dinner party (or out to dinner) versus when they're cooking for themselves at home. For that reason, I always advise preparing food that's exciting and a little indulgent. Leave your diet at the door.

Manifesting the Med

Cucumber Melon Spritzes
(PAGE 232)

Calabrian Tuna Tartare Toast
(PAGE 43)

Asparagus Fries with Feta
(PAGE 119)

Grilled Summer Veg
(PAGE 111)

Tomato and Spot Prawn Paella
(PAGE 165)

Lobster Capellini
(PAGE 148)

Butterflied Branzino
(PAGE 193)

Serves 6 to 8 people

For when it feels like everyone you know has transported themselves to a Mediterranean beach town and you're the only one who didn't get the memo. No need to pout, just invite some friends over, whip yourselves up some spritzes, and imagine you're at an Italian Beach Club. Except, unlike your Euro-tripping frenemies, you have access to ice and air-conditioning.

The Prep: Two days ahead, I would make the lemon aïoli, the sauces for the branzino, and the cucumber melon puree. The day before I would make the shrimp stock. The day of, I would prep the tuna first and have the tuna toasts ready for when guests arrive. I would grill the veg, cook the asparagus, and then cook the paella (but not the prawns) before guests arrive—serving the veg at room temp and reheating the paella in the oven. Then I would prepare the prawns, branzino, and the capellini simultaneously right before serving.

Hot Tip: This menu is the definition of maximizing your kitchen's capacity. We're roasting, barbecueing, baking, boiling, searing, and grilling. However, we still need to take into account our personal capacity, and since we can't do six things at once, we need another way. My secret weapon to stress-free hosting is serving as many room-temperature dishes as possible. This is because the most stressful moments of a dinner party are usually the fifteen minutes before sitting down to eat, when you're trying to get all of the food to the table at the same time while still hot. Remember, we're not contending for a Michelin star here, so pick your battles. I will always sacrifice my veggie sides to being served room temp if it means I can give my proteins my undivided attention.

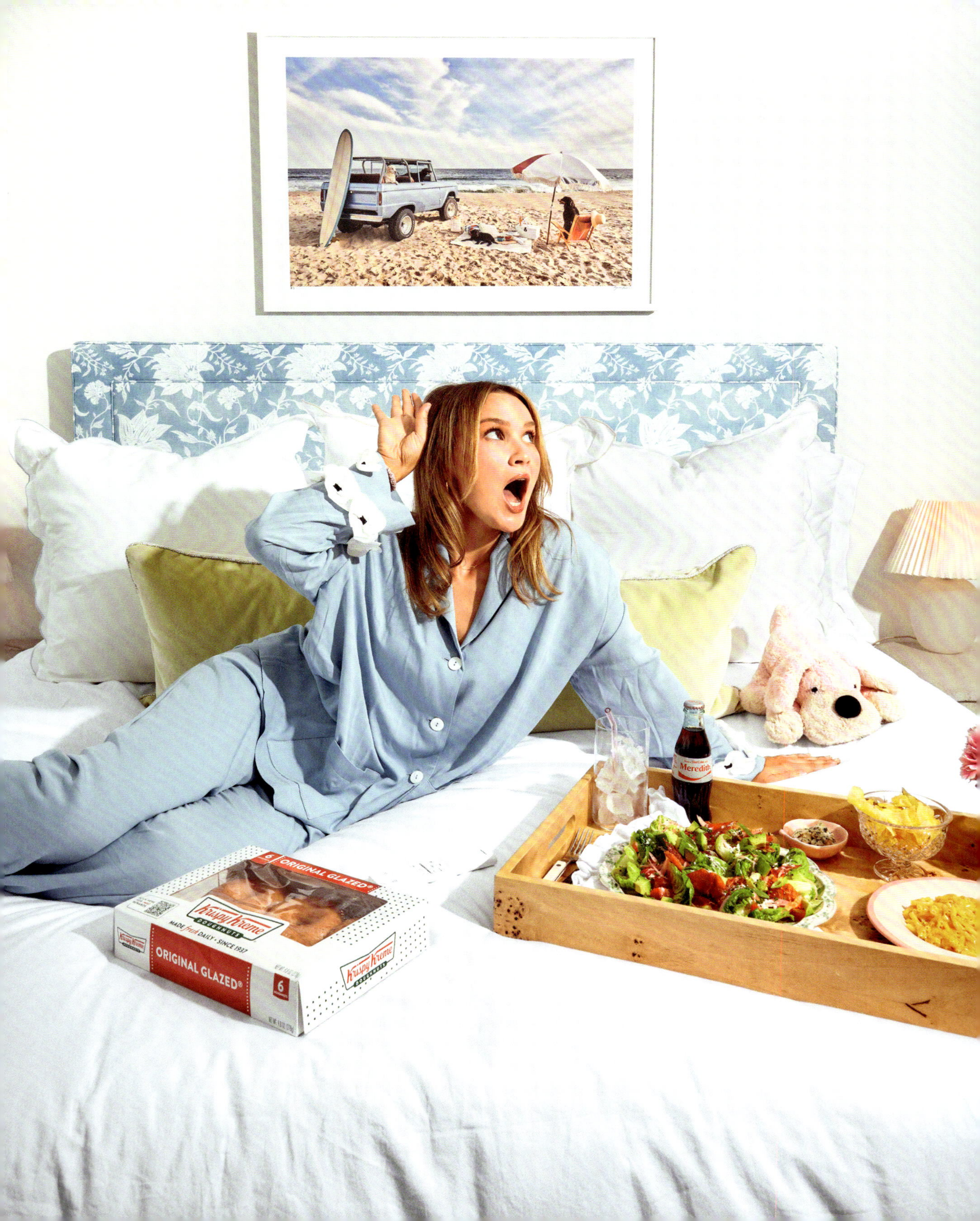
ORIGINAL GLAZED®
Krispy Kreme
DOUGHNUTS
MADE fresh DAILY • SINCE 1937
ORIGINAL GLAZED®
6
Meredith

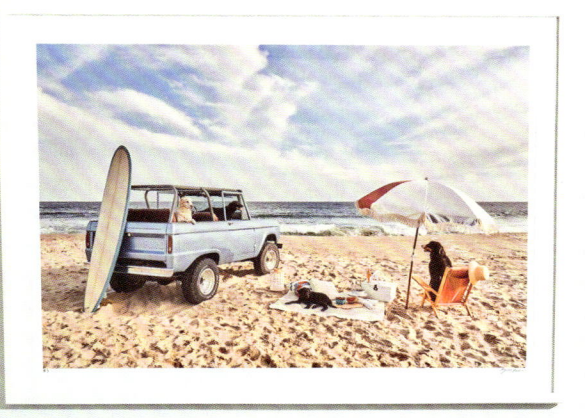

acknowledgements

To my parents, Tom and Nancy, and my brother, Tommy, for their constant support and encouragement.

To my agent, Janis, for giving me courage and confidence.

To my manager, Ali, for guiding me through every terrifying step of the way.

To my editor, Molly, for trusting my voice and my vision.

To my writer, Rachel, for helping me find my voice.

To my designer, Lizzie, for bringing our vision to life.

To my photographer, Emma, for perfectly capturing the essence of this book.

To my prop and food stylists, Pearl and Steph, for their patience and expertise.

To the production team, Terry, Jane, and Mari, for making the magic happen.

To my girlfriends, for always cheering me on.

To my Aunt Sue, for believing in me.

To my dog, Millie, for being my bundle of joy at the end of a long day.

To my first clients, Seth and Joseph, for taking a chance on me.

To my partner, Michael, for being my rock.

To my younger self, for putting in the work and never giving up.

To you, the reader, for giving me the opportunity to share my love of food with you.

I love you all so much.

thank you <3

meredith

index

A

Aïoli, lemon, 43
Anchovies, in Caesar crudités, 44
Appetizers. *See* Starters
Apple "pie" sundae, 255
Asparagus
    blanched spring veg, 108
    fries with feta, 119
    in squash ribbons with pistachio and pecorino, 59
Aubergine, in grilled summer veg, 111
Avocados
    in crispy fish with citrus salad, 190
    lobster avocado salad, 60
    in plt salad, 74
    really good guac, 36

B

Bacon
    bays, 48
    in chicken cutlet club, 97
Baking
    cathead biscuits and blueberry jam, 249
    deconstructed pie sundaes, 255
    heirloom tomato galette, 246
    olive oil cake with peaches and cream, 251
    s'mores ice cream pie, 256
    sticky toffee pudding, 259
Balsamic braised short ribs, 219
Balsamic vinaigrette, 56
    Italian chopped with buffalo mozzarella with, 56
Basil
    blueberry basil lemonade, boozy, 236
    parsley pesto, 144
        broccoli cavatelli with, 143
        heirloom tomato galette with, 246
        squash ribbons with pistachio and pecorino with, 59
        ultimate Italian with, 93
Beans. *See* Cannellini beans; Chickpeas

Béchamel, in chive crab cakes, 183
Beef
    balsamic braised short ribs, 219
    bucatini and meatballs, 131
    in harissa pitas with feta and cucumber, 215
    porterhouse with jammy tomatoes, 216
    short rib Bolognese, 141
    steak "tartare" sandwich, 105
Beer
    in fish tacos, 189
    in jalapeño michelada, 241
Berries, in summer fruit "pie" sundae, 255
    See also Blueberry
Bevs
    boozy blueberry basil lemonade, 236
    cucumber melon spritzes, 232
    dirty martini with blue cheese-stuffed olives, 223
    garden mere-y, 242
    jalapeño michelada, 241
    lambrusco negroni, 227
    passion fruit mezcalita, 235
    picante piña, 231
    pickled pepper martini, 224
    spicy salty ranch water, 228
Big fat Greek salad with souvlaki-ish chicken, 73
Birthday menu, 268
Biscuits, cathead, and blueberry jam, 249
Bisque, lobster, 83
Blenders. *See* Immersion blender
Bloody Mary. *See* Garden mere-y
Blueberry basil lemonade, boozy, 236
Blueberry bbq grilled chicken salad, 66
Blueberry bbq sauce, 66
    blueberry bbq grilled chicken salad with, 66
Blueberry jam, 250
    blueberry bbq sauce with, 66
    blueberry vinaigrette with, 66

    boozy blueberry basil lemonade with, 236
    cathead biscuits with, 250
Blueberry vinaigrette, 66
    bbq grilled chicken salad with, 66
Blue cheese
    in crushed olive spread, 52
    in plt salad, 74
    -stuffed olives, 223
        dirty martini with, 223
Bolognese, short rib, 141
Boyfriend roast chicken with pan-sauce potatoes, 204
Branzino, butterflied, 193
Broccoli
    blanched spring veg, 108
    brown buttered, 115
    cavatelli, 143
    roasted, with caper butter, 120
    salad, farro, 162
Brown butter vinaigrette, 77
    radicchio with hazelnuts and, 77
Bucatini and meatballs, 131
Buffalo mozzarella, Italian chopped with, 56
Burrata cheese, in heirloom tomato galette, 246
Butterflied branzino, 193
Buttermilk
    in cathead biscuits and blueberry jam, 249
    ranch, 74
        chicken cutlet club with, 97
        plt salad with, 74

C

Cabbage and herb salad, 69
Caesar crudités, 44
Calabrian chillies, 19
    Calabrian tuna tartare toast, 43
    red chilli sauce, 193
Campari, in lambrusco negroni, 227
Cannellini beans
    in Italian chopped with buffalo mozzarella, 56
    in ribollita, 80

Capellini, lobster, 148
Caper(s)
    butter, broccoli roasted with, 120
    in crushed olive spread, 52
    parsley caper salsa verde, 193
Carrots
    in not my mom's roast chicken, 199
    roasted winter veg, 112
Cathead biscuits and blueberry jam, 249
Cauliflower, chilli-braised, 123
Caviar potatoes, crispy, 51
Champagne vinaigrette, 65
    THE green salad with, 65
Cheddar cheese
    baked crab mac and cheese, 147
    in hot crab dip, 39
    pimiento-ish cheese, 39
Cheese
    baked crab mac and, 147
    homemade stracciatella, 35
    pimiento-ish, 39
    See also specific cheeses
Chicken
    big fat Greek salad with souvlaki-ish, 73
    boyfriend roast. with pan-sauce potatoes, 204
    in cabbage and herb salad, 69
    cutlet club, 97
    khao soi, 88
    lemongrass, & rice noodle salad, 156
    not my mom's roast, 199
    salad, blueberry bbq grilled, 66
    sandwiches, piri-piri, 101
    shake 'n bake, with hot honey tomatoes, 203
    soup, green garlic and ginger, 87
Chickpeas, in Italian chopped with buffalo mozzarella, 56
Chilli-braised cauliflower, 123
Chilli flakes, about, 19
    See also Sesame chilli crunch
Chilli-infused rum, 231
    picante piña with, 231

Chilli peppers. *See* Calabrian chillies; Fresno chillies; Jalapeño; Thai chillies
Chilli sauce, red, 193
Chive crab cakes, 183
Chocolate, in fudge, 256
Citrus, 19
    crispy fish with citrus salad, 190
    See also Grapefruit; Lemon; Oranges
Clambakes
    Nantucket, 176
    summer clambake menu, 272
Clams, in Nantucket Clambake, 176
Coconut milk
    in chicken khao soi, 88
    in green curry sauce, 98
    in picante piña, 231
Cod
    fish tacos, 189
    tomato butter baked, 180
Coriander
    cabbage and herb salad, 69
    citrus coriander salsa verde, 190
    in duck lettuce wraps, 207
    in lemongrass chicken & rice noodle salad, 156
    in tomatillo salsa verde, 213
Corn
    Nantucket clambake, 176
    tomatoes and, 116
Cornmeal, in pecorino polenta, 173
Country club menu, 275
Crab
    cakes, chive, 183
    fried rice, 161
    heirloom crab cocktail, 28
    hot crab dip, 39
    mac and cheese, baked, 147
Cream cheese, in hot crab dip, 39
Crudités, Caesar, 44
Cucumber
    harissa pitas with feta and, 215
    melon hugo spritz, 232
    melon puree, 232

    melon spritzes with, 232
    melon vodka spritz, 232
Curry paste. *See* Khao soi paste
Curry sauce, green, 98
Cutting boards, 14

D

Dates, in sticky toffee pudding, 259
Deconstructed pie sundaes, 255
Desserts
    deconstructed pie sundaes, 255
    olive oil cake with peaches and cream, 251
    s'mores ice cream pie, 256
    sticky toffee pudding, 259
Dinner party menus. *See* Making a menu
Dip
    for Caesar crudités, 44
    hot crab, 39
    See also Spread
Dirty martini with blue cheese-stuffed olives, 223
Dressing
    buttermilk ranch, 74
    feta, 215
    herb, 60
    See also Vinaigrette
Duck
    confit larb, 207
    fat potatoes, 124
    lettuce wraps, 207

E

Eggs, in crab fried rice, 161
Elderflower liqueur, in cucumber melon hugo spritz, 232
Entertaining. *See* Making a menu

F

Farro broccoli salad, 162
Fennel
    in lobster bisque, 83
    in pork sausage burgers, 102
Feta
    asparagus fries with, 119
    dressing, 215

Fish
- crispy, with citrus salad, 190
- tacos, 189
- *See also* Surf

Flaky salt, about, 17

Flounder, in green curry katsu sando, 98

Fresno chillies
- in chicken khao soi, 88
- in scampi shrimp, 185

Fruit, in summer fruit "pie" sundae, 255
- *See also specific fruit*

Fudge, in s'mores ice cream pie, 256

G

Galette, heirloom tomato, 246

Garden mere-y, 242

Garlic
- fried, ricotta with, 40
- green garlic and ginger chicken soup, 87

Gin
- boozy blueberry basil lemonade, 236
- dirty martini with blue cheese-stuffed olives, 223
- lambrusco negroni, 227
- pickled pepper martini, 224

Ginger, in green garlic and ginger chicken soup, 87

Goat cheese, in blueberry bbq grilled chicken salad, 66

A Good mash, 127

Graham crust, 256

Grains
- crab fried rice, 161
- farro broccoli salad, 162
- herby rice and radish salad, 170
- Mom's pilaf, 169
- pecorino polenta, 173
- tomato and spot prawn paella, 165

Grapefruit, in crispy fish with citrus salad, 190

Greek salad with souvlaki-ish chicken, big fat, 73

Green beans, in blanched spring veg, 108

Green curry katsu sando, 98

Green garlic and ginger chicken soup, 87

THE green salad, 65

Gruyère, in baked crab mac and cheese, 147

Guacamole
- really good guac, 36

Guanciale, in ziti zozzona, 137

H

Harissa
- pitas with feta and cucumber, 215
- seasoning blend, 112
- roasted winter veg with, 112

Hazelnuts, radicchio with, and brown butter vinaigrette, 77

Heirloom crab cocktail, 28

Heirloom tomato galette, 246

Herb(s), 19
- cabbage and herb salad, 69
- dressing, 60
- herby rice and radish salad, 170
- *See also specific herbs*

Holiday menu. *See* Winter holiday menu

Hot crab dip, 39

Hot honey, about, 19

Hot honey tomatoes, shake 'n bake chicken with, 203

I

Ice cream pie, s'mores, 256

Immersion blender, 14

Italian, Ultimate, 93

Italian chopped with buffalo mozzarella, 56

J

Jalapeño michelada, 241

Julienne technique, 70

K

Kale, in ribollita, 80

Khao soi paste, 88

Knives, 14

Kosher salt, about, 17

L

Lamb, in harissa pitas with feta and cucumber, 215

Lambrusco negroni, 227

Leek, in lobster bisque, 83

Lemon
- aïoli, 43
- Caesar crudités with, 44
- Calabrian tuna tartare toast 43

pork sausage burgers with, 102
- beurre blanc sauce, 183
- pink lemon pasta, 151
- vinaigrette, 111

Lemonade, boozy blueberry basil, 236

Lemongrass chicken & rice noodle salad, 156

Liqueur. *See* Campari; Elderflower liqueur; Passion fruit liqueur

Lobster
- avocado salad, 60
- bisque, 83
- capellini, 148
- Nantucket clambake, 176
- rolls, hot buttered, 94
- tutorial, 62
- wok lobster, 155

M

Mac and cheese, baked crab, 147

Making a menu, 264–65
- birthday, 268
- country club, 275
- manifesting the Med, 279
- pasta party, 276
- summer clambake, 272
- taco party, 271
- winter holiday, 267

Mandoline, 14

Manifesting the Med, 279

"Marshmallow" meringue, in s'mores ice cream pie, 256

Martini
- dirty, with blue cheese-stuffed olives, 223
- pickled pepper, 224

Mascarpone, in olive oil cake with peaches and cream, 251

Meat. *See* Turf; *specific types*

Meatballs, bucatini and, 131

Mediterranean menu. *See* Manifesting the Med

Melon, in cucumber melon spritzes, 232

Menus. *See* Making a menu

Meringue, "marshmallow," 256

Mezcalita, passion fruit, 235

Michelada, jalapeño, 241

Microplane, 15

Mignonette
- classic, 47

284 INDEX

yuzu kosho, 47
Mint
   cabbage and herb salad, 69
   in duck lettuce wraps, 207
   in herby rice and radish salad, 170
   in lemongrass chicken & rice noodle salad, 156
Mom's pilaf, 169
Mortadella, in ultimate Italian, 93
Mozzarella, Italian chopped with buffalo, 56
   See also Stracciatella

N

Nantucket clambake, 176
Negroni, lambrusco, 227
Noodles
   baked crab mac and cheese, 147
   broccoli cavatelli, 143
   bucatini and meatballs, 131
   lemongrass chicken & rice noodle salad, 156
   lobster capellini, 148
   pink lemon pasta, 151
   sesame chilli crunch, 136
   short rib Bolognese, 141
   spicy squash pasta, 135
   Sungold tomato pasta, 152
   wok lobster, 155
   ziti alla zozzona, 137
Not my mom's roast chicken, 199
Nuts and seeds. See Hazelnuts; Pine nuts; Pistachio

O

Olive oil, 17
   cake with peaches and cream, 251
Olives
   blue cheese-stuffed, 223
   crushed olive spread, 52
Oranges, in crispy fish with citrus salad, 190
Oysters
   oven shucking, 32
   Parm, 31
   with yuzu kosho mignonette, 47

P

Paella, tomato and spot prawn, 165
Pancetta, in short rib Bolognese, 141
Panko. See Toasted garlic panko
Pans. See Pots and pans, stainless steel; Roasting trays

Parmesan cheese, in basil parsley pesto, 144
Parsley
   basil parsley pesto, 144
   caper salsa verde, 193
   tarragon salsa verde, 199
      not my mom's roast chicken with, 199
Parsnip, in roasted winter veg, 112
Passion fruit liqueur, in passion fruit mezcalita, 235
Passion fruit mezcalita, 235
Pasta
   pink lemon, 151
   spicy squash, 135
   Sungold tomato, 152
   See also Noodles
Pasta party menu, 276
Pastry dough, 246
Peach(es)
   olive oil cake with peaches and cream, 251
   roasted peach salsa, 212
      pork tacos with, 212
Peas
   blanched spring veg, 108
   in herby rice and radish salad, 170
Pecorino
   in basil parsley pesto, 144
   polenta, 173
   squash ribbons with pistachio and, 59
Peppercorns, about, 17
Peppers
   chilli (see specific peppers)
   grilled summer veg, 111
   in ultimate Italian, 93
Pesto
   basil parsley, 144
   vinaigrette, 59
Picante piña, 231
Pickled pepper martini, 224
Pie crust. See Graham crust
Pilaf, Mom's, 169
Pimiento-ish cheese, 39
   hot crab dip with, 39
Piña, picante, 231
Pine nuts, in basil parsley pesto, 144
Pink lemon pasta, 151
Piri-piri chicken sandwiches, 101
Pistachio and pecorino, squash ribbons with, 59

Pitas, harissa, with feta and cucumber, 215
Plt salad, 74
Polenta, pecorino, 173
Ponzu sauce
   slow-roasted salmon with ponzu and sesame chilli crunch, 194
   in wok lobster, 155
Pork
   sausage burgers, 102
   tacos with roasted peach salsa, 210
   See also Bacon; Guanciale; Mortadella; Pancetta; Prosciutto; Sausage
Porterhouse with jammy tomatoes, 216
Potatoes
   crispy caviar, 51
   duck fat potatoes, 124
   a Good mash, 127
   Nantucket clambake, 176
   in not my mom's roast chicken, 199
   pan sauce, boyfriend roast chicken with, 204
Pots and pans, stainless steel, 14
Prawns
   scampi shrimp, 185
   shrimp stock, 166
      tomato and spot prawn paella with, 165
Prik nam pla sauce, 161
Prosciutto
   in Bacon Bays, 48
   in Italian chopped with buffalo mozzarella, 56
   in plt salad, 74
   in ultimate Italian, 93
Prosecco, in cucumber melon hugo spritz, 232
Pudding, sticky toffee, 259

Q

Quart containers, 14

R

Radicchio with hazelnuts and brown butter vinaigrette, 77
Radish salad, herby rice and, 170
Ranch, buttermilk, 74
Ranch water, spicy salty, 228
Really good guac, 36

Red chilli sauce, 193
   butterflied branzino with, 193
Red sauce
   classic, 132
      bucatini and meatballs with, 131
   in ziti alla zozzona, 137
Ribollita, 80
Rice
   crab fried, 161
   Mom's pilaf, 169
   and radish salad, herby, 170
   tomato and spot prawn paella, 165
Rice noodle salad, lemongrass chicken &, 156
Ricotta with fried garlic, 40
Roasting trays, 15
Rum, chilli-infused, 231
   picante piña with, 231

S

Salad(s)
   big fat Greek, with souvlaki-ish chicken, 73
   blueberry bbq grilled chicken, 66
   cabbage and herb, 69
   THE green salad, 65
   herby rice and radish, 170
   Italian chopped with buffalo mozzarella, 56
   lobster avocado, 60
   lobster tutorial, 62
   plt salad, 74
   radicchio with hazelnuts and brown butter vinaigrette, 77
   squash ribbons with pistachio and pecorino, 59
   tomato nuoc cham, 70
Salmon, slow-roasted, with ponzu and sesame chilli crunch, 194
Salsa
   roasted peach, 212
   verde
      citrus coriander, 190
      parsley caper, 193
      parsley tarragon, 199
      tomatillo, 213
Salt. *See* Flaky salt, about; Kosher salt, about
Sammies
   chicken cutlet club, 97
   green curry katsu sando, 98
   hot buttered lobster rolls, 94
   piri-piri chicken sandwiches, 101
   pork sausage burgers, 102
   steak "tartare" sandwich, 105
   ultimate Italian, 93
Sandwiches. *See* Sammies
Sauce, 193
   béchamel, 183
   blueberry bbq, 66
   green curry, 98
   lemon beurre blanc, 183
   mignonette, classic, 47
   mignonette, yuzu kosho, 47
   prik nam pla, 161
   red, classic, 132
   red chilli, 193
   tartare, 105
   toffee, 259
   tomato butter, 31
   See also Pesto; Ponzu sauce; Salsa
Sausage
   Nantucket clambake, 176
   pork sausage burgers, 102
   in ziti alla zozzona, 137
Scallops, in bacon bays, 48
Scampi shrimp, 185
Sea bass, Chilean, in crispy fish with citrus salad, 190
Seafood. *See* Surf; *specific types*
Secret sauces, spreads, and sprinkles, 20
Sesame chilli crunch, 136
   slow-roasted salmon with ponzu and, 194
   spicy squash pasta with, 135
Shake 'n bake chicken with hot honey tomatoes, 203
Shallots, quick pickled, 74
   chicken khao soi with, 88
   fish tacos with, 189
   hot buttered lobster rolls with, 94
   piri-piri chicken sandwiches with, 101
   plt salad with, 74
Shortbread crumble, 255
   deconstructed pie sundaes with, 255
Short rib Bolognese, 141
Short ribs, balsamic braised, 219
Shrimp *see* Prawns
S'mores ice cream pie, 256
Soup(s)
   chicken khao soi, 88
   green garlic and ginger chicken, 87
   lobster bisque, 83
   ribollita, 80
Souvlaki-ish chicken, big fat Greek salad with, 73
Spinach
   in broccoli cavatelli, 143
   in green curry sauce, 98
   in green garlic and ginger chicken soup, 87
Spread, crushed olive, 52
   See also Dip
Spring veg, blanched, 108
Spritzes, cucumber melon, 232
Squash ribbons with pistachio and pecorino, 59
   See also Summer squash; Winter squash
Starters
   bacon bays, 48
   Caesar crudités, 44
   Calabrian tuna tartare toast, 43
   crisp caviar potatoes, 51
   crushed olive spread, 52
   heirloom crab cocktail, 28
   hot crab dip, 39
   oven-shucking oysters, 32
   oysters Parm, 31
   oysters with yuzu kosho mignonette, 47
   really good guac, 36
   ricotta with fried garlic, 40
   stracciatella with marinated Sungolds, 35
Steak "tartare" sandwich, 105
Sticky toffee pudding, 259
Stock, shrimp, 166
Stracciatella
   in heirloom tomato galette, 246
   homemade, 35
   with marinated Sungolds, 35
   in ultimate Italian, 93
   See also Mozzarella
Summer clambake menu, 272
Summer fruit "pie" sundae, 255
Summer squash
   grilled summer veg, 111
   squash ribbons with pistachio and pecorino, 59
Summer veg, grilled, 111
Sundaes, deconstructed pie, 255

Sungold tomato pasta, 152
Surf
   butterflied branzino, 193
   chive crab cakes, 183
   crispy fish with citrus salad, 190
   fish tacos, 189
   Nantucket clambake, 176
   salmon, slow-roasted, with ponzu and sesame chilli crunch, 194
   scampi shrimp, 185
   tomato butter baked cod, 180
   See also Crab; Flounder; Lobster; Oysters; Prawns; Scallops; Sea bass; Shrimp

T

Taco party menu, 271
Tacos
   fish, 189
   pork, with roasted peach salsa, 210
Tarragon, in parsley tarragon salsa verde, 199
Tartare sauce, 105
Tequila, in spicy salty ranch water, 228
Thai chillies
   in chicken khao soi, 88
   in crab fried rice, 161
   in tomato nuoc cham, 70
Toast, Calabrian tuna tartare, 43
Toasted garlic panko, 31
   baked crab mac and cheese with, 147
   oysters Parm with, 31
Toffee
   pudding, sticky, 259
   sauce, 259
Tomatillo salsa verde, 213
   jalapeño michelada with, 241
   pork tacos with roasted peach salsa with, 210
Tomato(es), 17
   butter baked cod, 180
   butter sauce, 31
      oysters Parm with, 31
   classic red sauce, 132
   and corn, 116
   in garden mere-y, 242
   grilled summer veg, 111
   heirloom tomato galette, 246
   hot honey, shake 'n bake chicken with, 203
   in lobster capellini, 148
   nuoc cham, 70
      duck lettuce wraps with, 207
      lemongrass chicken & rice noodle salad with, 156
   porterhouse with jammy, 216
   in ribollita, 80
   in salads, 60, 74, 162
   and spot prawn paella, 165
   stracciatella with marinated Sungolds, 35
   Sungold tomato pasta, 152
   in ziti alla zozzona, 137
Tortillas, in tacos, 189, 210
Tuna tartare toast, Calabrian, 43
Turf
   balsamic braised short ribs, 219
   chicken with hot honey tomatoes, shake 'n bake, 203
   chicken with pan-sauce potatoes, boyfriend roast, 204
   duck lettuce wraps, 207
   harissa pitas with feta and cucumber, 215
   how to carve a chicken, 201
   not my mom's roast chicken, 199
   pork tacos with roasted peach salsa, 210
   porterhouse with jammy tomatoes, 216
   See also Beef; Chicken; Duck; Pork

U

Ultimate Italian, 93

V

Veg
   asparagus fries with feta, 119
   blanched spring veg, 108
   brown buttered broccoli, 115
   chilli-braised cauliflower, 123
   duck fat potatoes, 124
   a good mash, 127
   grilled summer veg, 111
   roasted broccoli with caper butter, 120
   roasted winter veg, 112
   tomatoes and corn, 116
Vermouth
   dirty martini with blue cheese-stuffed olives, 223
   pickled pepper martini, 224
Vinaigrette
   balsamic, 56
   blueberry, 66
   brown butter, 77
   champagne, 65
   lemon, 111
   pesto, 59
   See also Dressing
Vodka
   boozy blueberry basil lemonade, 236
   cucumber melon vodka spritz, 232
   dirty martini with blue cheese-stuffed olives, 223
   garden mere-y, 242
   pickled pepper martini, 224

W

Wine. *See* Lambrusco; Prosecco
Winter holiday menu, 267
Winter squash
   roasted winter veg, 112
   spicy squash pasta, 135
Winter veg, roasted, 112
Wire racks, 15
Wok lobster, 155

Y

Yogurt
   in Caesar crudités dip, 44
   in feta dressing, 215
Yuzu kosho mignonette, oysters with, 47

Z

Ziti alla zozzona, 137

CONVERSION TABLES

Recipes have been tested using imperial measurements and US cups. Conversions may yield different results. For best results, follow one set of measurements only – do not mix imperial and metric.

WEIGHTS

½oz	15g
1oz	25g
1½oz	40g
2oz	50g
3oz	75g
4oz	100g
5oz	150g
6oz	175g
7oz	200g
8oz	225g
9oz	250g
10oz	275g
12oz	350g
13oz	375g
14oz	400g
15oz	425g
1lb	450g
1¼lb	550g
1½lb	675g
2lb	900g
3lb	1.5kg

VOLUME

1fl oz	25ml
2fl oz	50ml
3fl oz	85ml
5fl oz	150ml
10fl oz	300ml
15fl oz	450ml
1 pint	600ml
1¼ pints	700ml
1½ pints	900ml
1 quart	950ml

MEASUREMENTS

⅛in	0.25cm
¼in	0.5cm
½in	1cm
1in	2.5cm
2in	5cm
3in	7.5cm
4in	10cm
5in	12.5cm
6in	15cm
7in	18cm

OVEN TEMPERATURES

140°C	120°C fan	275°F	Gas mark 1
150°C	130°C fan	300°F	Gas mark 2
160°C	140°C fan	325°F	Gas mark 3
180°C	160°C fan	350°F	Gas mark 4
190°C	170°C fan	375°F	Gas mark 5
200°C	180°C fan	400°F	Gas mark 6
220°C	200°C fan	425°F	Gas mark 7

Ebury Press is part of the Penguin Random House group of companies whose addresses can be found at global.penguinrandomhouse.com

Penguin Random House UK
One Embassy Gardens, 8 Viaduct Gardens, London SW11 7BW

penguin.co.uk | global.penguinrandomhouse.com

UK | USA | Canada | Ireland |
Australia | India | New Zealand | South Africa

First published by Ten Speed Press in 2025
This edition published by Ebury Press in 2025
2

The moral right of the author has been asserted.

No part of this book may be used or reproduced in any manner for the purpose of training artificial intelligence technologies or systems. In accordance with Article 4(3) of the DSM Directive 2019/790, Penguin Random House expressly reserves this work from the text and data mining exception.

Colour origination by Altaimage Ltd
Printed and bound in China by C&C Offset Printing Co., Ltd

The authorised representative in the EEA is Penguin Random House Ireland, Morrison Chambers, 32 Nassau Street, Dublin D02 YH68.

A CIP catalogue record for this book is available from the British Library

ISBN 9781529960266

Penguin Random House is committed to a sustainable future for our business, our readers and our planet. This book is made from Forest Stewardship Council® certified paper.

Acquiring editor: Molly Birnbaum | Production editor: Terry Deal
Editorial assistant: Gabby Ureña Matos
Art director and designer: Lizzie Allen
Production designers: Mari Gill, Faith Hague, and Merri Ann Morrell
Production manager: Jane Chinn
Prepress colour manager: Neil Spitkovsky
Food Stylist: Pearl Jones | Prop Stylist: Stephanie De Luca
Photo Assistant: Jon Scala | Prop Assistant: Esther Hwang
Food Assistants: Seth Boylan, Christina Chaey, Ava Chambers, Aaron Meftah, Courtney Presley, Christine Quach, Tia Rotolo, Sofia Swanson, and Kayla Wong
Copy editor: Patricia Dailey | Proofreaders: Miriam Garron and Rives Kuhar | Indexer: Barbara Mortenson
Publicist: Jana Branson | Marketer: Stephanie Davis